TWO JEWS ON A TRAIN

STORIES FROM THE OLD
COUNTRY AND THE NEW

TWO JEWS ON A TRAIN

Adam Biro

Translated by Catherine Tihanyi

The University of Chicago Press
Chicago and London

ADAM BIRO is a French art book publisher and author who was born in Hungary. His previous books include *Dictionnaire général du surréalisme et de ses environs* (coedited with René Passeron), *Loin d'où, Précis de musique charnelle, Quelqu'un d'ailleurs, Un rêve sur des landes désolées,* and *Tsigane.* CATHERINE TIHANYI is research associate in the Department of Anthropology, Western Washington University. Her numerous translations include works by Georges Duby and Claude Lévi-Strauss.

Originally published as *Deux juifs voyagent dans un train: Une autobiographie,* © 1998 Maisonneuve et Larose.

The University of Chicago Press, Chicago 60637
The University of Chicago Press, Ltd., London
© 2001 by The University of Chicago
All rights reserved. Published 2001
Printed in the United States of America

10 09 08 07 06 05 04 03 02 01   1 2 3 4 5
ISBN:0-226-05214-1 (CLOTH)

Library of Congress Cataloging-in-Publication Data

Biro, Adam
    [Deux juifs voyagent dans un train. English]
    Two Jews on a train : stories from the old country and the new / Adam Biro ; translated by Catherine Tihanyi.
        p.   cm.
    ISBN 0-226-05214-1 (cloth : alk. paper)
        I. Title.   Two Jews on a train.   II. Tihanyi, Catherine.
PQ2662.I733 D4813   2001
843'.914 — dc21   00-046718

When his students asked the wonder-rabbi of Budapest, Adam Biro ben

Mordechaï, if he was happy, if he wouldn't rather be a famous Jew like Moses,

Rachi, Maimonides, Marx, Freud, Kafka, or Einstein instead of Adam Biro, he

always replied: "When my time will come to stand in front of the Eternal God,

blessed be his Holy Name, he will not reproach me for not having been Moses,

Kafka, or Einstein. He will reproach me for not having been

Adam Biro ben Mordechaï of Budapest."

Contents

Translator's Note and Acknowledgments

I WOULD LIKE TO EXPRESS my heartfelt thanks to Adam Biro for his generous help with the translation process, his unfailing patience in answering intercontinental questions put to him through all the means of communication available in this beginning of the twenty-first century, and his thorough review of the final English text.

The author's voice was not easy to capture in translation. It is the voice of a storyteller, *telling* us narratives from an oral tradition, and at the same time it is that of a consummate writer steeped in French language and literature and delighting in the play of puns, alliterations, and the poetics of everyday discourse. But this French form is only one of the layers of this complex text that bears witness to both the tragedy and richness of the Jewish diasporic experience. As the author wrote me, "When I write, my pen pulls along Hungarian, Ashkenazi Jewish, German, French, and Sephardic Jewish French civilizations." Not all of this treasure fit comfortably into English. At times I had to find equivalent American cultural concepts and idioms rather than directly translate the French ones, and the author as well has slightly modified his text in some instances. As a result, the English-language text is at variance with the original French in a few places.

I would like to thank T. David Brent for entrusting me with this translation and for his helpful suggestions and comments, and Carol Saller for very ably editing the manuscript.

Introduction

THIS IS NOT THE STORY of my life, yet it is.* It tells that of two Jews traveling together on a train and talking with each other. They are traveling between Lemberg and Tarnopol . . . Well, not exactly; these towns have different names now. It was in the olden days, when there were still Jews . . . So let's say between Siófok-Tisztviselötelep and Leányfalu. (Or between Lyons-la-Forêt and Pont-aux-Dions, between Grange-Canal and Villars-sur-Glâne, Kyoto and Ishikozo, Tunis and Gabès, Ochsenzoll and Binningen, San Niccolo di Celle and Poggioventoso, between Anchorage and Juneau, between Saturn and Jupiter. Does it matter? They are everywhere and always on the road.)

Two Jews are traveling on a train. All Eastern European Jewish jokes start this way, or almost. When my daughters were going to school and they pretended to be asleep in the mornings so as to gain a few precious minutes and I ran out of arguments, I bent over them and whispered seven magical words very softly in their ears: two-Jews-are-traveling-on-a-train. The result was always the same: they couldn't help burst out laughing.

*This paradoxical opening renders the spirit of the original French title, which was *Two Jews on a Train: An Autobiography.* — Trans.

You might tell me: history, our history forbids us henceforth to speak of trains in a minor mode. They evoke horrible memories for Jews. But this quasi-traditional phrase that begins several of my stories dates from before, when trains brought no one to their death. Freud himself, in his study on jokes, gives us one of his famous examples: "Two Jews meet on a train at a station in Galicia. 'Where are you going?' asked one. 'To Cracow'. . . . 'Are you really going to Cracow, why are you lying?'"* In those days, journeys were interrupted with numerous stops and peddlers wandered on the platforms to sell pretzels, lemonade, and beer as travelers got off and on the trains: the train was a place of conviviality, of meetings, of exchanges, of happenings. Then a monstrous and stupid grayness arose and broke this image, and the rest.

Two Jews are traveling on a train. They are old and ugly, they are young and full of energy, they are silent and looking at the landscape, they are rich and they are poor, they keep on talking, they exchange banalities, trivia, crude words—all the world's pain, all the world's wisdom. Bottomless despair, joy of living, unspeakable misfortune of being, and also, there's the pride of being Jewish, an uncalled-for pride for an accident of birth. I don't resemble any of these people; I don't recognize myself in them—yet I know from the outset that one of these two Jews is me. And so is the other. These Jewish stories, of which not a single one happened to me, and of which I did not invent a single one, do describe me, do characterize me, do explain me. They are *always* my own story. And yours.

I am an open channel between the tellers of those stories and their listeners who will tell them in turn.

My main sources are five bound volumes, with yellow covers, belonging to my grandfather, my maternal grandfather, that is. (It's

---

*Sigmund Freud, *Jokes and Their Relation to the Unconscious,* ed. and trans. James Strachey (New York: W. W. Norton & Co., 1960), 115.

important I specify this because no one had less a feel for jokes than my mother, except perhaps my wife . . .) *Ötezer vicc* (five thousand *witz*), was published in Budapest, in another time, in another world, on another planet, before the war, yes, that war, the real one, the only one I experienced—up to now that is (we survived, God only knows how and particularly why).

And then there were other family sources.

My grandfather, whom I just cited, Dr. Luy György (1883–1960), who was the first, when I only knew how to listen, to impart to me the love of stories, whether they be Jewish or not. The famous yellow volumes of the *Five Thousand Jokes* were annotated and classified by him (he was a lawyer).

Hegedüs Nándor (1884–1969), the only one of my father's uncles to have survived the war. He was a dandy, a good-times ladies' man, extremely elegant even in Stalinist Hungary with his fur-collared coat and gaiters, a polyglot journalist of astonishing culture, as Eastern European intellectuals could be in those days. He was the director and owner of a daily paper at Nagyvárad in Transylvania, the friend and publisher of Ady Endre, the greatest Hungarian poet of the century. He held the post of Great Orator of the Freemasons of Hungary and was a representative of the Hungarian minority in the Bucharest parliament . . . He gave me my first book (the Hungarian translation of Mark Twain's *The Prince and the Pauper*) and it was he who taught me to love reading and writing. He imported all the stories from Nagyvárad to Budapest just so he could tell them to the ten-year-old boy I was at the time.

Bódi, his son, calls me from time to time from Basel, just to tell me a joke.

My father, whose favorite *witz* is "What is the difference between the Great Rabbi of Budapest and Napoleon? There isn't any: they both had a beard [at that point, my father always pauses dramatically, then he continues]—except for Napoleon" (and he looks at his audience as if he is a bowing actor awaiting applause).

Then there were friends, acquaintances, colleagues . . . But after first attempting to list them all, I had to give up. Those I would have forgotten would have been mad at me forever, and would have inflicted the most painful punishment on me: depriving me of jokes. And then there were readings: numerous, fortuitous, unruly.

But I would never have been able to tell you these stories without the tolerant, patient, indulgent, and compassionate presence of my daily victims, Karin, Julie, and Yaëlle.

I am finishing these stories at Tourtour, in the Var region of France, at the extraordinary Fondations des Treilles, where I was invited—welcomed, accepted. I look out the window on the last days of summer. This is the south of France, the weather is still sunny, warm; below, somewhere, lies the Mediterranean . . . Here, nature rules and a snow-winged peace drifts in the happy air . . . I am far, too far away from misfortune . . .

THE DELUGE

ONE DAY THE LORD . . . Whoa, hold on. Can we in the same breath thus speak of day, of time, and the incommensurable and incommensurate, the divine? No, we obviously can't. But can we then simply, directly speak of the Lord? No again. So let's go for it.

One day the Lord got fed up with humankind (some capitalize the word with an *H* as in Haman, Herod, Himmler, Hitler). Enough with human beings, He said. They are too smart to simply and divinely vegetate, so they get a fuzzy beginning of a grasp of some vague correspondence in the universal order. But since they are not intelligent enough to understand the whole, they doubt everything. There are more poor than rich, and God hates the poor. They don't love themselves and they don't love their neighbor; they are too mean to each other, thus they are always suffering. They are too unhappy. In a word, they are imperfect.

I have to admit I made them badly. That's no problem, though; there are enough creations in the Universe: comets, stars, planets, galaxies, solar systems, and all sorts of animate and inanimate things. This one is a failure. I don't want to think about it anymore. I am doing away with it.

And the Eternal God sent His angels to warn human beings: "In ten days a flood will cover the earth, and all traces of humankind will disappear."

Indescribable panic took hold of all the nations, all people. This time, there was no appeal. Priests were preaching: "This is the righteous punishment for all your sins." Politicians accused their opponents, heads of state their neighboring countries, scientists their colleagues who had rejected their theories, parents reproached their children for not having followed the path they should have, children reproached their parents for having taught them useless things, artists thought that if their works had been understood they would have saved the world, neighbors blamed neighbors, brunettes blamed blondes, misogynists blamed women, misanthropes blamed everyone, atheists blamed believers, believers atheists, both blamed God—only lovers wholeheartedly gave in to their pain without blaming anyone.

The president of the most powerful country on earth, the United States of America, was notified of the divine threat in the middle of the night. He felt awful. He knew he was constantly living in sin; he was greedy, arrogant, pretentious, full of himself, a liar, merciless to his enemies, cowardly when facing the strong, and, under his leadership, the country had accumulated all the imaginable sins with which God could reproach men and women. Moreover, his country was crushing the other countries of the planet, with no other justification than that of its wealth. And wasn't this very wealth the main reason for the divine ire?

He gathered all his advisers, each one of them meaner and more selfish than the other. They were unanimous: this was serious. No interplanetary weapon, no bomb, no secret plane could save America. The most advanced technology would be useless. Even when the president was told that the boss of the biggest computer company in the United States, thus in the world, was asking to see him, he refused even though he had worshiped for years the ground that person walked on. He now knew that even the most advanced computers were going to be less useful than a true word, a glance, or a pebble at the bottom of the pond.

He took his car, after dismissing his chauffeur and bodyguards, who were anyway in the process of packing to return to their own homes, and he went to his native village in the north of the U.S. He parked his bulletproof car that was immune to any assault at the edge of a small wood where he used to play as a child. He wandered for hours, remembering all the meadows, all the ponds, all the trails, all the places where he had been happy once, a long time ago, and he was infinitely sad.

"I wanted to be the leader. I wasted my life," he told himself. "And now, it's too late."

During his walk he understood what could still save Americans from their announced end. He thus went back to the White House, where no one was left. Guards, police in civilian clothes, secret detectives in uniforms, secretaries, bureaucrats, cabinet ministers, all had gone back to their families. Doors and ultrasecret drawers were open; offices were as empty as the streets and public squares. He called all the presidents of the TV channels at their homes—he realized how useless it was to have so many. He told them that he intended to make a historic speech. The word "historic," just when history was definitely ending, made the people he was talking to laugh, but nonetheless they did send out crews to spread his message. It was not easy to get technicians to show up, as they had no interest left in presidential *scoops*.* And yet, they did come, because one never knows . . . Americans are a hopeful, positive people.

The president gave a speech that moved all the television audience. (In spite of everything, television had such a power in this country that, even in these tragic times, most of the people kept on watching the tube.) They said to themselves, "If the president had made this sort of speech during his inauguration, the world would have had a different fate."

---

*In English in the French text. In order to convey some of the flavor of the original, all such non-French expressions will be italicized in the English text as if they were foreign words.— *Trans.*

The president of the United States first announced the end of the world in a neutral and measured tone.

Then he beseeched his fellow Americans to put to good use the ten remaining days and change their ways, love their fellows, and do as much good as they possibly could.

"Give away your wealth, your money, your jewels, your stocks, your artworks, your clothes, your food, your land, your animals, your cars, your houses, all your possessions, to those poorer than you. And don't think it's useless. Go out in the street and forgive your enemies, hug them and invite them into your homes. Go to theirs if they invite you. I am sending all the members of the armed forces back to their homes and I have given the Pentagon the order to immediately destroy all weapons belonging to the state, and I beg you to do the same with yours. Only love and goodness can save us, if there's still time. May God have mercy on our country."

When the president of Russia heard the news, his first reaction was to keep it secret. But it was too late. Everyone had heard the voices of the angels. People were watching foreign television, cable channels; they listened to radio from other countries. To silence the news was no longer possible; only denial, negation was still conceivable. But the president was suddenly seized with great fatigue, with immense tiredness. It was exhausting to constantly lie. He had been lying ever since he'd come to power. What am I saying! He had been lying well before, so as to get to power. He was exhausted. He was a believer. He was certain the angels' message was true; the world was going to end. He wasn't going to prevaricate. The Russian president decided that enough was enough, and he longed for the glory to be the first statesman (and the last) since the creation of Russia by the Vikings to tell the truth to the people. He had all the programs on all public and private television stations and radios in all the autonomous republics of the Russian federation interrupted so he could make a solemn declaration.

His speech was preceded by Gregorian chants, then a series of spotlights were turned off one by one and then came back all at once much brighter than before, all aimed at the standing president.

With a quasi-triumphant tone, with the air of someone who has just won a great victory, he ordered all the owners of clothing stores, all the sellers of perishables, of wood, of heating oil, of coal, all the owners of restaurants and taverns to immediately open their establishments and let everyone help themselves to whatever they wanted. He gave permission to all the people under his jurisdiction, to all the citizens, to clothe and heat themselves, to eat and drink to their hearts' content.

"The time has come, before the end of the world, for you, I mean for us, to dress ourselves and to eat our fill after enduring one thousand years of deprivation. Eat, drink, dress, warm yourselves, make your body happy, even if only for the last time. Do not end your lives in pain and misery; be warm and satiated as you pass on."

In France, no one made any speeches; no politician thought to make a solemn declaration. Nobody would have listened to it. People despised politicians and they had better things to do. Subways, trains, planes, taxis, cars were full, crowded with people and under attack by others wanting in. It was the same with sidewalks and country trails. All the population was running around in a panic, trying to say for the first or last time *Ich liebe Dich* to someone.

As for the Jews, they drew lots among the president of the World Jewish Congress, the president of the Jewish Agency, the Great Rabbi of France, a Reform American rabbi, an Orthodox Russian rabbi, the three prime ministers, four presidents, and five Great Rabbis of Israel (all officiating at the same time), and Frantisek Finkelstein, grocer in Prague, to decide who would go on the air to announce the news of the deluge to Jews. The one who drew the highest number made a very short speech. He addressed the people, the whole of the Jewish people, as follows:

"Jews of the whole world! You have ten days to learn to live under water."

FISH HEAD

TWO JEWS ARE TRAVELING on a train. In an old train *k.*
und k., kaiserlich und königlich, imperial and royal. That's the way
trains were called in the bicephalous Austro-Hungarian empire.
Trains, stationmasters, schools, gas and running water on every
floor, the army, the secret police, sewer drains, court advisers, ministers—everything official was imperial and royal. Even wars. Espe-
cially wars. Until one day or another, in 1918, there was no longer
any *k*, nor *k*, nor emperor, nor king. (They were, you might have figured out, one and the same person. The *k* of the Austrians and
of everyone else, those somewhat inferior beings, Bessarabians,
Ruthenians, and what have you, and *k* of just the Hungarians, this
since the historic Compromise of 1867. And the *k* of the Hungarians even learned their language. Late in life and poorly, *k*lunkity
*k*lunk, but as Hungarian *k* he had to. Could you imagine the *k* of
the French not being able to speak French? Not to mention that the
k of the Hungarians lived in a foreign country, in Vienna. And that
Romy Schneider—the pseudonym of *Madame* Sissi, the *k*'s wife,
spoke it better than her husband, yes, this impossible Asian-like
sort of idiom. But she, she had her reasons: she had a Hungarian
lover. Did she learn Hungarian from him? Did he speak his mother

tongue to her in bed? Did he whisper it in the imperial ear of Elizabeth von Wittelsbach, legitimate spouse of Franz Josef of Hapsburg, emperor of the bicephalous remains of the defunct Roman-German-Holy-Empire, now only encompassing Austria, Bohemia, Slovakia, Ruthenia, Moldavia, Bukovina, Galicia, Dalmatia, Bosnia-Herzegovina, the Sandjak of Novi-Bazar, Croatia, Slavonia, Moravia, Silesia, Tyrol, Styria, Carniola, and a few other dependencies? Did he whisper obscenities from back home to the spouse of the king of Malta, the Protector of Jerusalem, the Apostolic King of Hungary—did this *Magyar lover* utter swearwords in the language of the herdsmen of the *puszta* at the supreme moment of pleasure? Or did the good woman in love learn Hungarian in secret to please her aristocratic lover, the minister of foreign affairs *k*-imperial and *k*-royal? We shall never know, too bad.)

Two Jews were traveling on a train *k. und k.* It was before the Great War that separated the Belle Epoque (that of the cuckold emperor and that of the even more cuckold empress) from the period that followed, less beautiful from a purely aesthetic viewpoint. (I didn't have the opportunity to participate in this war, but my grandfather talked to me about it, with regrets in his voice. He regretted having allowed a Russian bullet to deprive him of the use of his right arm. He regretted not having photographed my mother, as a little girl of four, seated on the throne of the king of Serbia, in Belgrade occupied by the Austrian army. But I had the privilege to know the next one, the next world war that is, so I have nothing to regret.)

Two Jews are traveling on a train, in second class. To travel in first class would have been a useless expense, as they are of moderate means. As for third class with its wooden seats, only peasants and workers use it. There are only three travelers in the compartment. The two coreligionists and, facing them, a young officer *k. und k.*, of relatively low rank, a lieutenant. He's a sample of this famous Hungarian army which, first under the commandment of *k. und k.*, and then completely independently, succeeded and was to succeed in participating in all the wars that occurred in the neigh-

borhood—the First, the Second, and no doubt the Third when its
time comes—and, under the creative leadership of strategic ge-
niuses, succeeded in losing them all, with no exception or hesita-
tion. This famous army, led by humanists who have always found
one or more good reasons to cause without any regret the massacre
of hundreds of thousands of peasants and workers. The only army
in the Danubian basin which, guided by clever diplomats, has always, I mean always, sided with oppressors, then losers: Austrians,
Germans . . . The next episode is bound to be predictable.

One of the Jews is my maternal grandfather. He is already
Catholic, not that this is noticeable. He has already given up his
birth name, that of his father, a poor seltzer tank delivery man, Finkelstein Jenö, for his brand-new name, Luy György, that of his
adoptive parents, moderately well-off Transylvanian nobles who
helped out his parents unable to raise him.

It's already past noon and the two Jews are hungry. They open
their bags and pull out their meager lunch wrapped in wax paper.
Some small dried fish, onions, bread, a bottle of red wine. That's
all. But all that stuff smells very strong and very bad. They are hungry; they gobble up their food, eating without any manners, swal-
lowing everything, every which way, without any order, as they are
speaking. They splutter, spit out the fish bones. One of them even
eats the fish heads while his fellow puts them aside but doesn't
throw them away. He carefully wraps up the remaining heads in the
paper and then puts them back in his bag.

The officer, plump in his superb white uniform, looks disgusted. The smell of fish mixed with that of the onions is unbearable. But driven by curiosity he says nothing, as he is visibly
intrigued by his travel companions. He fidgets, he coughs, clears
his throat, opens the window, pulls open the curtains, asks for
permission to do so . . . He gives the impression he would like to
start a conversation, but doesn't know how to go about it. And then
mustering his courage and stifling his disgust, he asks them where
they are going. He is a man of the world, but not the world of the
two coreligionists. He tells uninteresting stories of military life, he

brags, he wants to impress the two Jews who would become canon fodder if trouble should break out but would not be allowed to be officers. He makes small talk. It is obvious that he has something else on his mind. His neighbors answer politely, bored. And then suddenly, he finally asks them the question that is troubling him:

"Tell me, how come you Jews are so intelligent, so much more intelligent than the rest of us?"

"Are you sure of that?" ask the two others in unison.

"Oh, yes! I have observed this a thousand times in my village and in Budapest when I was there. And everyone knows it, everyone says it; it's a well-known, proven, fact. There are thousands of anecdotes about this. Even you, you spread this rumor yourselves, because you feel superior to others and superior in intelligence. Where does this pride come from, and from where do you get your famous intelligence?"

My grandfather answers in a conspiratorial tone.

"It's a secret. Only Jews know it. They never reveal it to anyone. I don't have the right to tell you. We have more than enough problems; we're the butt of too much grief already. The only thing we still have is our intelligence. If we didn't have at least that, we would have already ceased to exist. Everything can be taken from us, our money, our possessions, our wives, our children; we can be driven away, but there are two things that cannot be taken from us, even under torture: our faith and our intelligence. So . . ."

(My future grandfather was bragging. He had at the time neither wife nor child. As to faith . . . Some years later, in order to marry my future grandmother, who was very pious, he had to reconvert to Judaism and learn Hebrew and the Talmud. In this way, this sole member of my family to be truly and totally an atheist was also the only one to have extensive religious knowledge.)

The officer understands that he is experiencing an important moment. He offers them money.

"Tell me your secret. I'd like to become intelligent like you. I'll pay for it."

"And you swear to never tell it to anyone?"

"I swear it!"

"And if you were to tell anyway? How would we know? You would cause us grave harm as the other Jews would chase us away from the community and then everyone would become intelligent, and then, woe on us!"

"If the sacred word of an officer isn't enough, here's my name, my address. If ever I should talk, you could come to my home and avenge yourselves. Name your price; I'll not haggle."

The two friends consult each other in Yiddish.

"Okay. You seem honest, truthful, we trust you, we trust your word as officer of the heroical and victorious imperial army. That will be one thousand pengös."

The sum is enormous. The lieutenant swallows and breaks into a sweat, but agrees.

"Now tell me."

"The secret of our great intelligence lies in fish heads. You have certainly seen Jews eat fish heads. Even the poorest ones. That is precisely why even the poorest among us know how to read, write, and pray. It's thanks to fish heads. They contain phosphorous, springtosis, cretinitus, cortemarine, and many other elements that develop the brain's capability. And moreover they were blessed by our ancestor Moses in the Sinai Desert during the *Meshüge,* the feast of the blessing of the fish heads."

The officer is impressed. He would never have thought of it, and yet it's evident. All of these wretched Jews he encounters during exercises in the inns of the monarchy and who are eating sprats, herrings, carp . . . so that's why!

He pulls out his wallet and pays. The two buddies share the money, and there's silence. Suddenly one of the Jews gets the hiccups.

The officer is deep in thought. The hiccupy Jew suddenly stands up and runs out to the hallway accompanied by his friend, who is slapping him violently on the back. Then the other one comes back, but as soon as he enters the compartment, he is seized with such a terrible fit of coughing that he has to leave again immediately.

The officer, who is now a holder of the millennial secret, can hardly wait to arrive at his destination to try the new panacea, the miracle cure against stupidity. He had seen one of the Jews pack away his uneaten fish heads. As soon as the two come back, the lieutenant addresses him:

"You've some fish heads left; I've seen you put them away. Give them to me."

The poor Jew's horrible cough starts up again, and he has to leave again to expectorate. He must have tuberculosis, thinks the officer. The other Jew remains, very unhappy-looking.

"How do you expect us to give them to you? We just explained to you that it is our vital sustenance. Our intelligence, our only possession that allows us to live, needs to be sustained and fed all the time. If we give you this secret food, we would be headed straight to our own destruction."

The officer thinks some more, as evidenced by his wrinkling brow, his sweat, his tics. Where, when I get to my destination, am I going to find fish heads? Nowhere. I will have to wait for my next leave, for God knows how long, to go to town and buy some. And then where could I find a quiet spot to eat them? There is not one inch of privacy in the barracks . . . But here—that would be perfect. The heads are at hand, and he can eat them without being seen, in peace, without his fellows making fun of him.

"Sell them to me," he says, almost begging.

His interlocutor has to go consult his friend. (This is still my grandfather. He became, much later, after the First World War and its inconveniences, a lawyer in Budapest, a one-handed lawyer, shrewd, rich, stubborn, tough, and with his heart in left-wing politics . . . Then World War II came along with its own brand of inconveniences. After the Russian soldiers of the tsar had deprived him of the use of his arm, Hitler took his money and Stalin his practice—but not his high spirits, or his fatalism.)

The two Jews are co-owners of this special food. My grandfather goes out in the hallway, then comes back alone, and tells the officer that just for him, and since they already gave him the key to the secret, they have agreed, as a most rare exception, to divest themselves of the precious heads. And they are asking only four hundred pengős for them.

"That's a week's pay," thinks the officer, but right away he takes out his money and gives it to the Jew, who then hands him the parcel wrapped in paper and hurriedly leaves the compartment.

The officer immediately starts to eat the miracle food he had so yearned for. No matter its smell, its look, the gross contact with the small viscous heads. He proceeds to chomp on them, conscientiously, one by one. He is not only disgusted but he becomes nauseous. He keeps on chewing with his eyes closed—all of a sudden nausea takes hold of him and he can't go on. These heads with their small round eyes are truly gross. As he is alone in the compartment, he lets out a painful burp. He looks out the window and has the urge to vomit. The lieutenant, now turned white as a sheet, attempts to resist, takes deep breaths. Well, I am not eating any more of them. I've had it. That's too bad, but they are really uneatable. He is feeling sick. He needs to stand up, to take a few steps. He grabs the package of fish heads and throws it violently out the window and then he bursts into the hallway, where he bumps into the two buddies in the process of telling each other something very funny, slapping each other on the knees and shoulders. The cough of the man suffering from tuberculosis has completely disappeared. Upon seeing them, the officer, furious, red in the face, yells at them:

"I can't stand it anymore! I've thrown your fish out the window. I don't know how you can swallow those disgusting things. I can't do it. They are gross and they taste horrible. How dare you ask me four hundred *pengős* for this filthy stuff. You tricked me shamelessly! You're filthy thieves! It's downright robbery!"

My grandfather Finkelstein-Luy Jenő-György left-wing-Jew-Catholic-Jew-atheist-Talmudist mockingly points his finger at the officer:

"Look! You can see that we didn't trick you at all. On the contrary! The proof is that you've almost understood everything. You're already in the process of becoming more intelligent!"

FATE

[I]

THE TISZA IS FLOODING, yet again. The Tisza, the
biggest river in Hungary next to the Danube, flows serenely, when
it is calm, that is. Then its current is slow, regular, and peaceful. But
before its shores were built up, it could run wild and swallow up
everything. Everything: the living and the dead, plants, trees, fields,
gardens, people and animals, houses and their contents. It un-
earthed cadavers along with their coffins as raging rivers are in the
habit of doing.

I don't know the Tisza very well. I was born on the shore of the
Danube, a river that I hate. The Tisza represented for me the deep
country, the true Hungary of the true Hungarians. (I mean by that:
of all those who lived in Hungary, all except the Jews. In vain we
had lived there for centuries, in vain did we claim to belong to that
land . . .) It represented the province and the countryside, in con-
trast to the Danube, which, flowing through capitals such as Vienna, Budapest, Belgrade, stood, in my eyes as a child, for the city,
urbanity, and cosmopolitanism. It was only when I became an
adult that I discovered that one of my grandfathers, my paternal

one, the one I associated with mountainous Transylvania and the city of Nagyvárad—the mythical Nagyvárad, so urbane, so civilized, brilliant, and Jewish—where he was the director of the large Jewish high school, that this grandfather originated from a small village on the shore of the Tisza, in deepest Hungary, where his father, my great-grandfather, had been a schoolteacher. (This grandfather Biró, whom I had actually known, rests—how inappropriate this expression—at the bottom of the Danube. Hungarian Nazis threw him in with his son, my uncle, in January 1945. Oh God, how can I be writing this, just like that? Human beings did this. To a high-school principal and a historian of art. Yes. They did it before, after, in Europe, in Africa, in America, everywhere. We know their arguments, even their names. They are among us here, too, today. They never die. They wait for the next opportunity. I know their names; their puffed-up faces sully our eyes riveted on the television screen or on the front page that one of the newspapers complacently offers them. And us? What are we waiting for? How can we keep on living, keep on bearing this? How can I keep on telling stories, here, to you? Over there, that was my family . . . And even if . . . It's almost the same thing in the end . . .)

The Tisza was flooding. It was in the nineteenth century. A year of sunshine, of good harvest. And suddenly, the terror of this immense mass of water. The Tisza was only water, but it wiped out all the wheat, the bread of the people, along its way, with an end-of-the-world noise of total destruction.

People were running away. They knew; they had heard about it in the past. They had heard of the fury of the peaceful river, of the death it could sow.

Everyone was fleeing, except Izsák. The muddy water had already flooded the basement of his house; the vegetable garden was also under water. His family, his wife and children, had gone to visit his in-laws in a town thirty kilometers away, far from the Tisza— luckily. They were safe.

Izsák, seated in the parlor, was praying. Around him panic, calls, screams. The church bells were frantically ringing the alarm. There was mooing, animal cries.

Izsák prays fervently. A boat, filled with people, comes close to the open window. Mózes and Smuel are rowing with all their might. They call up:

"Izsák, come. What are you doing? The village is under water; we have lost everything. God is punishing us harshly for our sins. Come, there's still room for you. What on earth are you waiting for?"

Izsák, unperturbed, looks upon them disdainfully.

"I am praying. Leave me alone. I am praying to my God. He will save me."

The people in the boat look at him, flabbergasted. Izsák has always behaved a bit weirdly. But now he seems completely nuts. Can't he see the water inexorably covering everything? He doesn't stand a chance . . . But he tells them to leave him and to keep on going. They do leave; what else can they do . . .

The Tisza doesn't calm down; on the contrary. The tops of trees now stick out of the water, and the waves of the river are twirling wardrobes, cribs, and ripped-out doors, bumping them against each other through a bizarre law of chance. The stiff, already swollen bodies of animals are carried by the current. Izsák has to go up to the second floor of his house, as the ground floor is flooded. The furniture with all the family clothing and linen, the fruits of a life of work, the beautiful carpets given by his in-laws are all prey to the out-of-control element. Izsák doesn't care. "Mere objects," he says. He has nothing but contempt for "objects," for "things." He was told, he was taught, to value and be interested in only the spiritual. Who cares about old wooden chairs? Why should he worry about them? He is surely not going to sacrifice his faith, his trust in God, for a few old shirts? What is he going to take with him to the other world on the day of his death? Chairs or his soul? His family is safe; that's important. As for the rest. . . .

Another boat nears the house. Izsák knows all its occupants. People from the village, his neighbors.

"Izsák, are you still here? You must come; it's awful what's happening. The whole village has been carried away by the flood. We have never seen anything like this, such a violent flood, never. Come quick! We can't wait long—we have to go save others."

Izsák waves them away.

"I am praying to my Lord, the Eternal God. He has never abandoned me. You, you impious, bad believers, do what you wish. You are putting your trust into a lousy rotten rowboat rather than the Lord. You think you can save yourselves on your own instead of asking the Lord for help. Do what you want—go away, let me pray."

But the water keeps on rising. It breaks the window of the bedroom; screaming, hissing, it fills the room. It deposits a sticky greenish mud on the sheets, the pillows, the pristine white bedspread, before lifting up the massive solid wooden bed, making it gyrate like a toy top and slamming it against the ceiling. The flood, having done its duty in the bedroom, then rushes into the attic. Izsák barely has time to take refuge on the roof.

It is then, at that precise moment, that a new boat comes by. It approaches Izsák with difficulty. All that can be seen from the village are the tops of a few trees, a few roofs, and the church spire. It was once a village; it is no more . . .

The people in the boat yell from afar:

"Izsák, you've gone mad! You'll die for sure! There is no one left in the village—you are the only one, the last! Come with us, we are coming, just jump in the boat!"

But Izsák, clinging to the chimney of what had been his house, insults them.

"Me, yes, I alone, I am praying to God, who looks at me, who recognizes me, and who will save me, without you. I don't need you, you men of little faith, that's for sure."

The people have neither time nor desire to argue with a madman. They want to save their lives and leave this doomed village. Too bad for this poor idiot. There's nothing they can do; perhaps he will make it on his own. They leave, tossed by the current, in the boat piled up with men, women, children, animals, mattresses, cooking utensils, clothing, and useful and useless possessions.

And the black water keeps on rising. It tears Izsák away from his chimney. The poor man desperately tries to swim, but the current is stronger than he is. He struggles, swims, disappears, comes back up, spits out water. His breath gives way, he tries to cling to the pieces of furniture the current spins as it carries them along, he goes under again, and he drowns.

Right after . . . or rather, immediately, without delay—there is no delay in the time of the other world—Izsák is standing, dry and clean, in front of the Lord. He remembers perfectly well, but with celestial peace and calm, his last minutes of life, his hopeful struggle, his desperate drowning, the horror of his death . . . and he addresses his God, as prophets used to do, in these words:

"Lord, I don't understand You. The whole village fled, without waiting for Your will. The synagogue was empty the moment the catastrophe began. I was the only one, yes, the only one, to have prayed, to have looked to You. I put my faith and my life into Your hands. I *knew* You were going to save me. Only You could save me . . . and look, Lord, what You did to the village's only believer: You drowned him!"

God's infinite wisdom might have been shaken if it had not been divine and infinite.

The Lord looked upon Izsák with pity and told him:

"My poor Izsák, I too don't understand you. Why didn't you trust me? In vain, I sent three boats to save you!"

∀ ∀ ∀

There are several morals to the story you have just heard. First, it shows the humanity of Jewish wisdom. He who lacks faith in mankind, who refuses his or her human condition, who rejects solidarity with the community, doesn't deserve to be saved. The path to God lies in the solidarity of human beings. And, then, history proves that God lets you freely choose your fate. (I speak as if I were a believer. Bravo! It's almost believable . . .)

I know another version of the same story. Identical, although . . . Listen.

[I I]

Young Max Haddad was very ugly. It happens, even with French Sephardic Jews. They are all thought to have a Rolex on their wrist and leather jackets opened to show Lacoste shirts themselves opened at the neck to show a *magen David* (in Central Europe, amongst real Jews, it's pronounced the right way: *mogen Dovid*), that is, a golden Star of David on a chain (of the same material) around the neck. They are all thought to drive Porsches, and they all, without exception, live in Neuilly (sur Seine),* one of the ritziest nouveau riche neighborhoods in Paris. But how wrong can you be! Believing all those clichés will land you headfirst into the snares of platitudes. Max, for instance, lived in Belleville, a modest working-class area, and got around on the subway ("got around" might be an exaggeration: mornings, he went to work; evenings, he went back to his garret). He was poor and, moreover, hideous and deformed. His face was pockmarked, pitted, pimply . . . no woman would have caressed him, kissed him. His forehead was low, his thick black hair almost merged with his eyebrows, his ears were tiny but stuck out, his nose was shiny, his lips were so thin as to almost disappear, his shoulders drooped . . . Let's skip the rest, except for his hunchback, which couldn't be ignored. One would have had the right to wonder why God had punished him so. This much misfortune seemed unjust. Max suffered from this state of affairs. And when we say suffer . . . But how would you have reacted if you had been this unfortunate and awkward young man in the flower of his youth, with a head filled with ideas and images of women?

But fate (fate? Hmm . . . where does it live? How can one meet it?) took pity on him. I who know everything (of course, as I am the creator of all this, of this world, the world of these stories), I tell you that he met his fate in the tobacco shop of rue Saint-Antoine, at the corner of rue Caron, in Paris, in the Marais [the swamp], the Jewish

---

*There are other "Neuilly"s around Paris but not a single one is like Neuilly-sur-Seine . . .

neighborhood of Paris where Max was in the habit of filling in the numbers on his lottery ticket form while drinking a mixture of instant bouillon and white wine (never order this!). On a Wednesday, Max filled in his ticket as usual, paid for it and his drink—and, to his amazement, the next day while watching TV, he found out he had won several hundred thousand francs.

I don't intend to describe the poor man's happiness in detail, his outburst of joy, his unfortunate calls to his parents, to his few friends and colleagues (they resulted in requests for loans, dues, help, gifts, and subsidies in numbers far greater than that of his acquaintances). No, my purpose is not to describe Max's well-deserved happiness (—so, winning the lottery deserves our respect now?), but to continue with his fascinating story.

Max had suddenly become wealthy.

After the above-mentioned phone conversations, after giving money to those who didn't need it and refusing it to the needy, he began to think about himself.

"I'm going to make myself handsome," he said to himself, and he inquired about the address of the best plastic surgeon.

This creator, this reconstructor of being, turned Max Haddad I into an unrecognizable Max Haddad II, one with a very *in* haircut above a cleared forehead, ears, still small but discreetly hugging his head, lips as they would appear in a *chewing gum* ad—and mostly and miraculously, a torso and a back fit for an athlete, with no hump and hollow!

Max had suddenly become handsome.

(Stendhal would have been happy; he too openly envied and secretly despised the beautiful along with the wealthy people.) Now handsome and rich, he became self-confident. The poor and shy, short, hunchback Jew turned into a triumphant dandy (oh, come on, nowadays you call that a *playboy!*). His sure, dancing gait, the way he projected himself forward, the feline rowing motion of his shoulders as he walked, his quasi-haughty bearing, his virile handshake impressed men and seduced women.

He bought himself a leather jacket, Lacoste shirts, a big golden chain with a six-branched star, a Rolex, and a sports car whose make you could never guess. And to show his independent spirit, he moved into the sixteenth arrondissement of Paris, the other ritzy nouveau riche neighborhood.

One day, shortly after his many surgeries and his miraculous transformation, he had to go to the United States on business (he had been offered numerous very well paid jobs, as it is well known that only money can attract money, and that money is lent only to the rich, and while failure is an orphan, success has a large family . . . Do you wish me to tell you more gems from the wisdom of nations?). He thus flew to New York, where he concluded a business deal, a very juicy one, and where he made the acquaintance of a brunette, a very fleshy one. (That's the way Max liked them. He had simple and immediate tastes—that is, if you understand what I mean by "immediate," 'cause I don't quite understand it myself. At any rate, it's not the most appropriate adjective to qualify the substantive "taste" with.) They liked each other (the adjective and the substantive as well as Max and the fleshy woman) and promised to join their lives together. Max decided to settle in America, as he understood that it was there that "it was happening," and that it was there that *you can make it*. America was made for him, and the new Max, the with-it Max, was made for America, for its infinite possibilities, for its freedom of doing and succeeding. To succeed! To succeed! At what, where, specifically why—it didn't matter, what mattered was to succeed! This word vaguely meant money, riches—no matter—succeeding was enough in itself.

Max had to go back to France to take care of some formalities before definitely settling in New York. His fleshy, burning woman had promised to wait for him, him and his success.

But fate would have it otherwise.

Max's plane exploded in flight, off Nova Scotia. Years of investigation could not ascertain the cause of this accident. All the passengers and the crew died—let us hope they died quickly, painlessly.

And then, right after . . . or rather, immediately, without delay—there is no delay in the time of the other world—Max is standing, dry and clean, in front of the Lord. He remembers perfectly well, but with a celestial peace and calm, his last minutes of life, the horror of his death . . . and he addresses God, as the prophets and Izsák the Hungarian had done, in these words:

"Lord, I don't understand You. You punished me so harshly for all the sins of humankind: You made me born in a poor family and, not satisfied with this, You created me ugly, deformed, hunchbacked. And yet I was as innocent as any newborn. And You made me miserable. And You knew it too. How many times I prayed to You, but You didn't listen to me. And then chance changed my destiny. All of a sudden I became someone else: rich, then handsome. And at the very moment when I can finally fulfill all of my desires, at the moment when I meet the woman of my life who returns my love, at the moment when I can settle down to found a family in a country of peace and happiness, You kill me . . . !"

God listens to Max, then he looks at him closely, and finally says:

"What, is this you, Max Haddad? How silly of me—I didn't recognize you."

AT THE ROTHS'

AT THE END OF THE LAST CENTURY there lived in Vienna a famous and proud *schnorrer,* the king of professional con men, a fast-talking beggar talented in extracting money from people without ever actually putting his hand out. He was in fact more a *Luftmensch* than a *schnorrer,* that is, a man living from thin air whose sources of income were either unmentionable or unimaginable. His name was Roth.

It was a blessed time. Europe knew (biblically) peace and enjoyed it. Everyone had work, except for the unemployed, who didn't exist (since they were not accounted for in any statistics, or listed in any list . . .).

Roth had a good heart. He successfully dealt with his own affairs, which was a duty. He was feeding his family very well by borrowing from Peter to pay Paul, by extorting pitifully small sums from strangers with promises of incredible returns, by investing minute sums of his friends' money into nonexistent though nonetheless highly risky stocks. One of his specialities was horse races. He always claimed to have heard the very surest tips from the horses' mouths themselves, and he put the money from the bets he thus generated into his own pocket without any compunction. And yet, he was dishonest only out of necessity and out of ignorance of any sort of moral code of conduct, because at bottom he was a good guy. Once his own needs were satisfied, he helped out if he could whoever asked him to.

Like for instance this poor Finkelstein. He had been unemployed for years; in fact, no one had ever seen him work, or look for work. This did not prevent—or rather, this did leave him the leisure to constantly make his wife pregnant. He vegetated in a slummy basement room in the Wolfgasse; they were six in a room and a half that smelled of all the odors of the Creation, and without any hope of a saving breeze. The latch on the sole tiny window was broken and Finkelstein, fearing becoming dizzy, did not dare climb on a stool to fix it, so there was no possibility for any draft to make its way into the dark, earthen-floor shelter. In vain would I attempt to describe the children's clothes, the state of their health, the furniture in the hovel. In vain would I try to render the vocabulary the parents used to talk to each other, to reconstitute the daily occupation of the members of the family. On these matters, I have to refer the reader to great nineteenth-century specialists such as Dostoyevsky, club president, or Zola, chair of the troublemaking committee. Finkelstein lived off petty thievery, expedients, and odd jobs he did for his neighbors. His wife cleaned houses and took in laundry.

Roth knew Finkelstein, but of course Roth knew everybody. While he looked down on him for his lack of resourcefulness, his shunning of responsibilities, his alcoholism, his spinelessness, his indolence, he felt sorry for his children and his wife, who had done nothing to deserve their fate. One day, seeing Finkelstein headed toward the watering hole known as "Dead Man's Wash," an establishment famous for the elegance of its clientele, the distinction of its staff, the refinement of its interior decor, and the quality and choice of the available drinks, Roth, moved by his coreligionist's halting walk and by his raggedy clothes, addressed him as follows:

"Finkele, would you like me to introduce you to the baron Rothschild?" His interlocutor was flabbergasted:

"You mean you know him? You mean you think he might . . ."

"I'm sure of it. Money weighs heavy on the wealthy. They suffer from it. They know they don't deserve it any more than the poor deserve their empty wallets and tough ends of months—and people as wealthy and thus as intelligent as the Rothschilds know that they'll be naked in the grave. And anyway, they are only Jews like you and me—when we crossed the Sinai Desert, surely we slept in the same tent! Come on, I'm taking you to the baron; he'll take care of you."

"But let me first go home, change, and wash . . ."

"Absolutely not! You must awaken his compassion, his pity! Come as you are, au naturel."

The Rothschilds deserve a special chapter in the history of Jewish histories. They represent much more than money, riches, success, power. They personify the state toward which all Jews must strive. Actually, it's a normal state; one that all Jews should have by right, if only there were justice in this world. The Rothschilds don't exist; they are but symbols, abstractions. And anyway, no Jew has ever met them. Everyone knows they have been created by other Jews, for internal use. They live only in stories. The baron with his torn jacket at Gstaad who refuses to change because everyone who knows him knows he can afford to buy two thousand other ones, and those who don't know him don't matter. The Rothschild family traveling and paying a fortune for an omelet in a restaurant because, while eggs are in plentiful supply in this country, Rothschilds are not. The Rothschilds visiting the queen of England, at a funeral, at the racetrack; one of the many barons of the English branch seen in Paris with a *goy* floozy . . .

Thus Roth and Finkelstein are on their way to the baron Rothschild (to "the baron": he has no given name. They are and have always been barons; their motto: "Won't stoop to be prince, can't be king, thus the baron Rothschild I am"). There are a number of persons waiting in front of the palace, some dressed like Finkelstein, some much better, holding briefcases and looking busy. The liveried majordomo has them enter one by one, each time after a brief conversation. Roth pushes everyone aside with an authoritarian

and slightly brusque wave of the hand; his uncomfortable and ad-
miring protégé in tow. At the door Roth barks at the majordomo:

"Bar Roth, from Roth *und* Roth. We have an appointment with
Herr Baron. We are already late."

And without waiting for a reply, he pushes open the door and enters the foyer and then the waiting room.

Some of the visitors, elegant, gloved, and perfumed, are seated
on gilded Empire-style chairs and couches upholstered in cashmere. Others, poor-looking, wearing caps, are standing. Among
the latter is Count Ganef von und zu Kassenleerer, the finance minister of the monarchy.

The twelve-foot-high door opens from time to time and a secretary, a monk dressed in a cowled robe of rough serge, calls in the
next person. Roth, taking advantage of the exit of the ambassador of
the Sublime Gate and of his secretary, throws himself toward the
twelve-foot door and the monk, and announces:

"Roth,"

and, dragging Finkelstein behind him, enters the baron's study.

This latter is dressed in a smoking jacket made of *ikat,* the pure
silk speciality of Jewish weavers of central Asia, and his head is covered by a *kapele* crisscrossed with silver threads. He is seated behind an enormous gilded and lacquered rosewood desk, and even
as he gives the intruders a terribly tired and bored look, he keeps on
counting the pile of diamonds on his desk. He puts the biggest one
to his left, in a bag of red velvet decorated with the intertwined letters BaRo. The midsize ones go to his right, in a blue brocade sack
decorated with a crown. As for the little ones, a casual sweep of his
hand sends them flying to the wastepaper basket or onto the floor.
A multicolored parakeet swings on the Venice crystal chandelier,
white bearskins overlay Persian carpets and, on the wall, paintings
by the old masters face paintings of the ancestors. Through the
glass door giving onto a luxuriant garden, sunny in spite of the fall
season, one can make out young maidens in white and pink and big
hats promenading and to whom a bald servant, with sideburns and
handlebar moustache, is offering refreshments.

Roth pays no attention to the decor and directly addresses the head of the dynasty, who isn't bothering to raise his eyes a second time.

"Herr Baron, I am Bar Roth, and I represent the house Roth *und* Roth. You must have heard of us. I am taking the liberty of recommending to your proverbial kindness and generosity our unfortunate coreligionist, Zebulon Finkelstein. He suffers from heart disease, has arthritis and horrible ulcers in his stomach, and has been without work for years because of a hernia aggravated by a double helicoidal fracture of the fibula that has disabled both his arms one hundred and twenty percent. His wife died, leaving him a widower with seven young children of whom three have tuberculosis. They are surviving through gifts from the Hevra Kadisha, the Zohar, and the parasha, and the pension I give them monthly. The results of the last two transactions my firm conducted were not as good as previously—well, you know how that is, you are also in business—and I have the greatest difficulty with taking care, in addition to my own large family and my other protégés, of the education and feeding of the thirteen Finkelstein children. I am thus calling upon Herr Baron's legendary generosity: please help this unfortunate man, help him to bravely bear his poverty, as he . . ."

The baron Rothschild, the hundred and thirtieth of that name since the exodus from Egypt, still in the process of sorting out his diamonds, waves in the direction of the door, where his secretary is standing with a pad of paper in hand.

"Make a note, Dom Irenneus. One hundred each month."

Finkelstein can't believe his ears. He throws himself on the baron's right hand, covering it with kisses and in the process causing a dozen big diamonds to fall to the floor.

"May the Eternal God . . ."

The baron interrupts him. "Enough," he says while pulling out his hand with evident disgust. "Thank you Mister Kinkelnot, *goodbye.*"

The monk grabs the crying Finkelstein by the shoulders, pushes him toward the door, and calls the next visitor in.

When the Russian minister of war and peace entered bowing as required by the etiquette of the court at Saint Petersburg, that is, by clicking his heels and bending his torso at a right angle even while raising his head at another right angle and holding his bicorne hat on the small of his back with his right hand while placing his left one on the spot where up to age thirteen he still had a heart, the baron Rothschild, lifting his eyes to the Russian acrobat, realized that Roth was still in the room.

"What do you want now?"

"Herr Baron, we are not through yet. I brought you some business—how about my commission?"

THE TRAVELING
SALESMAN

To the memory of the great Karinthy Frigyes,
from whom I have stolen this story's punch line shamelessly—
on the contrary, proudly.

TWO JEWS ARE TRAVELING on a train. On a train between two stations and two wars, in Czechoslovakia, at the time it still existed. It's complicated. I warned you: don't listen to these stories from Eastern Europe. They'll depress you. When they are not complicated, they are absurd. When they are not desperate, they are incomprehensible. And if you do wish to understand this one, you'll also need to read a history book, or better yet, look through the atlas *Les Frontières européennes de 1900 à 1975: Histoire territoriale de l'Europe* [European borders from 1900 to 1975: The territorial history of Europe] (Geneva: Editions Médecine et Hygiène, 1976), compiled by Aldo Dami, former professor of political, historical, ethnic, and linguistic geography at the University of Geneva.

The two Jews in the train have no need of a manual. They know it by heart, the history of the center of Europe—as for borders, what a joke! They were born Austrians at Pressburg, it had become Pozsony by the time they had to prepare their secondary school exams, which they had to do in Hungarian (what bad luck . . .), then it turned into Bratislava and they became Czechoslovakians, and they'll die in the same place one day as very old Slovaks (if they're allowed . . .)—all this without ever leaving home—what could top that!

Two Jews are traveling on a train. They start out not knowing each other, but, very soon, they make each other's acquaintance. They talk about their families. They tell each other *witz*. They are silent for a while. Where are they going? And why? They fall silent again, each trying to think of a relative the other one might know. They do find them, a whole bunch of them, in spite of their obvious difference in social class. This is because this difference is only appearance. Finally, they speak of their respective occupations. One, Dr. Schwartzvogel, is a dentist; the other, Mr. Saphir, is a sales representative. They used to be called *wiegehts* because a traveling salesman when introducing himself used to say in German: *wie geht's? How do you do?*

"What are you selling?"

"Everything for the home. But I don't do retail. No door-to-door, I only deal with retail establishments. They know me in the whole of the country. I've done this for more than twenty years . . . so, you can see . . . I started well before the war . . ." (For the benefit of younger listeners: this war was the first, the one referred to as the "Great.") "Did you hear about Goldzieher *und* Goldverberger? Ah, dear Sir, what a business that was! I had everything, from shoe polish to rope, from hair and mustache nets to nacre buttons . . . and not just a couple of spools of thread, I am telling you . . . the smallest shop would order twenty . . . while the biggest notion stores in downtowns would order them by the hundreds. But today, what can I tell you? It's miserable. Nothing sells anymore. I travel because I like to travel. And because I have a wife and two kids, and my daughter is pregnant and her husband is out of work, and my son is still a student . . . So we all need to eat." (The surprised, incredulous reader might identify this lament as the age-old one handed down from the *Canterbury Tales*, 1387, through the *Farce de maître Pathelin*, 1464, and the *Crise du livre*, by the Parisian bookseller Baillères in 1904, and through the April 30, 1947, issue of the *Républican lorrain*, and the publisher Jérôme Lindon's article in *Le Monde* of June 10, 1998: the lament "everything used to be better before.")

Dr. Schwartzvogel can only agree: he has many fewer patients than in the past. People have fewer toothaches, or they no longer take care of them. They'd rather suffer. Some die for it; the doctor knows them well—they'd rather die than give their money to the dentist.

And so they while away the time. But there's no idle time for Mr. Saphir. Everyone is a potential customer.

"*Herr Doktor,* I told you I only work wholesale. Never retail. I am not one of these puny beginning salesmen. With my work and experience I only do wholesale. And then I'm too old to drag along a bunch of suitcases filled with merchandise. But I like you. I'm tempted to break my rule and let you benefit from a brand-new novelty I am presenting for the first time to my best customers, and only to them. It's to reward them for their loyalty to me, to let them make some money thanks to good old Mr. Saphir. Do you have bugs in your home?"

"What bugs?"

"You name it: cockroaches, fleas, lice?"

"What are you thinking? In the home of a doctor?! I demand complete hygiene! Disinfectant in my office, castile soap in the toilets . . ."

The *wiegehts* interrupts him:

"Of course, but in summer, wasps, bees . . .?"

"Never!"

"How about flies," begs Saphir.

"No!" exclaims Schwartzvogel.

"Grant me a few mosquitoes," sighs the other, almost crying. "In Bratislava, there's lots of mosquitoes. It's the river; you know, the Danube. It's sheer hell, unbearable. You can scratch till you bleed.

And the children, the poor children, covered with bites, what a shame."

The doctor accepts the mosquitoes. Those little beasts that enter through open windows during summer nights. Though at any rate not so much in town as in the countryside.

Saphir, grateful, grabs at the straw. He wastes no time on provincial mosquitoes. Upon discovering that the doctor's family often goes to the countryside, near Nemeckovice, he surreptitiously reintroduces all the other beasties the doctor chased away a few minutes earlier. Oh, insects make a country holiday almost unbearable, and then re-enter the bees, but mostly the wasps, ants, hornets, bumblebees, chiggers, ticks, my God, how dangerous they are, they can cause meningitis, and then re-re-enter the flies . . . but, luckily, Saphir is here; how lucky for the doctor Schwartzvogel that he took the same train as he, and can you see how sometimes God looks out for us, rarely, but when he does, he does it well, they are in the same compartment, alone, which makes it possible for Saphir to privately show the doctor Schwartzvogel his latest item, even before the large establishments of the downtowns have to refuse it to some of their overeager customers.

"It's a revolutionary method to kill insects. More powerful than DDT or any other powder, surer than flypaper. The rate of success is one hundred percent. Yes, *Herr Doktor.* I am telling you, one hundred percent. Let me explain."

And he pulls out from his large, visibly well-traveled suitcase, a brand-new elegant leather case with two copper latches. He opens it proudly to show polished steel boxes containing some wooden objects.

"You see, *Herr Doktor,* it's very simple. See, this is stick A-B. The letters are engraved on the two ends by a special pyrographic engraving process, patented in the United States Congress by the firm Hohgipfel *und* Niederloch of Ceske Budejovice. You place the harmful insect you wish to kill (allow me to use this term that is a bit strong, a bit cruel, but they deserve it for all the trouble they cause us) on point C. I'd like to draw your attention to the quality of the wood, specially made from a rot-proof African tree whose import is strictly controlled and reserved for the firm that holds the world patent for the device. Then—are you still following?—you carefully pick up with your fingers stick D-E, let me see how you do it, perfect, but carefully, though anyway, this wood too is imputrescible, can you imagine! You lay stick A-B across stick D-E so that they form a ninety-degree angle, or a cross if you prefer. Point F of the D-E stick, there, you see? must be superimposed over point C of the A-B stick. In this clever way, the insect is caught between the two sticks. Then you take this clamp made of a steel specially brushed by a technique specially invented for this use, a technique called "antiskid," patented worldwide. You insert into the preset grooves of the clamp the cross made by the superimposed sticks A-B and D-E at their intersection point. You check the firmness and stability of your device, and you impart two *usque* three [*wiegehts* are fond of foreign words] circular movements with your left or right hand, depending on whether you are left- or right-handed, to the small winged nut whose wings have been marked G-H by the same engraving process used on the wood, but this time applied with a slight variation to the special steel of the clamp. Once this circular movement is completed, you wait one or two minutes—if I might, based on my several years of personal experience in the matter, I would advise waiting two minutes rather than one. Then you carefully but purposely unscrew the winged nut G-H; you lift it, you pull apart the two sticks A-B and C-D, excuse me, D-E, and on the intersection point C, you will find the dead insect. The insect's death is guaranteed in writing by the manufacturer in the enclosed document. Then, you pick up the insect with a piece of gauze located in a special compartment of the case, and you throw it away. If you find yourself in a place devoid of trash cans, you put the gauze-wrapped insect in receptacle I, made of sterile antithermic glass, till you find a trash can. That's it. It's guaranteed for life, yes, for life, as I told you. And as to the price, I can make you one, just for you . . ."

The doctor Schwartzvogel, who had patiently followed Mr.

Saphir's presentation, is no longer listening. The traveling sales-man notices this immediately. The doctor has been in deep thought for several moments. Then suddenly, he raises his head and asks out of the blue:

"Your device is very interesting. But tell me, Mr. Saphir, could you not just squash this insect by hand?"

Mr. Saphir is silent, he scratches his chin for a good while, and then says, as he wrinkles his forehead, raises his eyebrows, and low-ers the corners of his mouth in profound disappointment for the wasted time and in scorn for the complete lack of understanding of his interlocutor:

"Squash it? Why not? It's another method . . ."

THE FOX

IT HAPPENED IN THE OLD COUNTRY. (As they say, because there are still those, either very old or very stupid, who say "the old country," just this way, with a touch of nostalgia. They could almost add "ooh, those were the good old days." But really! The shtetl, the pogroms, the mud, the filth, the superstitions, the ignorance, the poverty . . . the good old days in the good old country. And yet . . . the past embellishes everything. I was a bad high-school student, and miserable to boot for all sorts of good and bad reasons. And when I think again of my high-school years of which I so eagerly awaited the end, the disappearance, the obliteration, the death, well, when I think of them now, I *could* cry, but I don't cry, because men don't cry, that is, real men of course, winners, unfettered by inner feelings . . . The type of man I am not but would like to be, and, thank God, I'll never be.)

Thus it was in the old country. At a time when there were still real winters, great colds, real snow, really scary forests, endless steppes, when people were still hunting. And don't you dare laugh! Don't tell me that Jews didn't hunt. That's not so. I had plenty of them in my family—that is, hunters, yes, peasants too, landowners with fat Hungarian mustaches, and boots, and who, once or twice a year, brought to the city a smell that hadn't come from *schul* but from the earth and the animals, along with bottles and provisions I suspect might not have been kosher, not one bit, and that were incredibly delicious, real, homemade, grown, picked by these fat smelly Jewish peasants in all respect identical to any fat smelly peasant of the old country. They thus went hunting as any other fat peasant would.

The story I'm telling happens during one of those cold, snowy, foggy days when only hunters, their dogs, foxes, and wolves leave the warmth of the hearth to venture in the deep and snowy forest. (In the paradisal old country—which gets increasingly paradisal as I get deeper into this story, a story into which I sink as into the forest snow of the old country—even wolves had well-heated fireplaces.) It was in the course of one of those perfect days typical of tales of the old country that Kohn comes across his best friend on the village square, his friend from birth, his childhood buddy, Grün. This latter had all the accoutrements it takes to be a true hunter: rifle on his shoulder, knife in his belt, cartridge box for cartridges, game bag for game, meat bag for meat, visor for vices, teeth bag for teeth . . . Whatever! I wouldn't know; I've never hunted. I hate hunters, except those from the old country.

"Where are you going, Grün?" asks a smiling, half-curious, half-worried Kohn.

"Can't you tell? I'm going to the synagogue!"

Kohn was quite surprised. "You're going to the synagogue armed the way you are?"

"Kohn, you know full well we are not allowed to bring weapons into the house of God. You can see I'm going hunting. Why are you asking me such a stupid question?"

"What, you Grün, a good Jew, you're going hunting? Don't you know that it's very dangerous? Aren't you thinking of your family? Your wife? Of Rachel, your eldest daughter who needs to be married soon? You're scaring me, Grün. And what are you going to hunt: hares, partridges?"

"My poor friend, I don't know where you live, I don't know

where you're from, and I don't want to know. I don't know you. I have never met you before, only today, for the first time—and the last. Because I don't plan on meeting you ever again. Come on, partridges in January? Why not antelopes and sea lions? There's plenty of them in January in our woods! Oh well, I'm only going to tell you because you are insignificant, a *niemand,* a puny *azes ponem* on his way out of my life: I'm off to hunt fox."

Kohn sits down on the edge of the fountain from which, given the cold, no water is surging, and puts his head into his warmly gloved hands.

"*Oyweh tsores,* Grün. I am your friend and I'm afraid. Not for you but for your family. The fox is a very dangerous animal. First, he can attack people; he can bite if he feels cornered without any hope of escape. Worse, he can piss on you, and his urine can be deadly if it's from a female with a liver disease. What will you do if you miss, if you shoot to the side, if you aim badly, if the animal moves when you shoot? It can jump on you, bite you, kill you instantly, or piss on you and you'll die later if it's a female with liver disease."

"Kohn, you king of the *meshüge,* just think how much bad luck I'd need for, at the same time, aiming to the side, the beast moving, it attacking me instead of running away, it happening to be a female, and moreover a sick one, and moreover one suffering specifically from a liver disease, and moreover one just needing to pee, and moreover me letting her piss on me—don't you think that's a lot of 'ifs'? But even if I grant you, because I am sick and tired of arguing with you and I'm in a hurry to go hunting as I explained to you, if I grant you that it's possible I miss the first time, I will just shoot again."

"So," replies Kohn, "what if you miss again? First, you are clumsy, and then if you missed once, there is no reason not to miss a second time, a third, even a fourth time."

"The reason would be that to the contrary I'm a great shot. If I missed it the first time it would be because it moved. I'll just wait for the right moment and then, bang!"

"And bang, what if you miss it anyway? It will be enraged, beside itself, fearing for its life, it will feel it has nothing to lose—for sure it will jump on you."

"So, I'll run . . ."

"But Grün, you are so naive, or you're doing it on purpose; a fox runs very fast, much faster than a man, and particularly much faster than you! It will catch up quickly with you and then, *schniack*, his teeth will be in your calf or, worse, in your throat . . ."

"Then, *schniack*, I'll climb a tree . . ."

"You really think a fatso like you will succeed in climbing a tree . . . But all right, assuming this happens, he'll then quietly wait for you at the foot of the tree, and you'll be done for . . ."

"I'll hit it with the butt of my rifle!"

"And what if you dropped your rifle when climbing the tree?"

A heavy silence falls on the two friends. Grün is deep in thought. He must be weighing all the possibilities, all eventualities. Then, looking Kohn in the eye, he says:

"Tell me Kohn, whose friend are you anyway, mine or the fox's?"

THE TIME OF DAY

TWO JEWS ARE TRAVELING on a train. An old one and a young one. An old rabbi and some sort of student of the Talmud. They are alone in the compartment. The rabbi wears a fairly elegant felt hat with a large brim. He has a well-cared-for beard; no specific religious clothing, no side curls, the sort of rabbi Hungarian Jews would call "neologist"—a "modern" rabbi. He is reading from a well-worn prayer book, one that has been read and reread a thousand times. He reads out loud in a muffled voice, and stops from time to time. During these pauses, he either raises his head from his book with a vacant look or checks the big gold watch he pulls from his vest pocket and which is attached by a thick gold chain to one of his buttons. At those times, his eyes meet those of the other passenger seated opposite him, obviously a lot younger than himself, poorly dressed, with a threadbare jacket from which stick out the fringes of his *tales koton,* a clean white shirt with a collar made almost transparent by countless washings and ironings. The young man reads as well, also with a muffled voice; he is studying like his elder. Their voices mingle, blend, turn into the buzzing zum-zum bzz-bzz of a wasp. They do not speak to each other. Suddenly, the young man, almost as if coming out of a dream, almost as if coming from another world, looks in horror at the landscape through the window and addresses his traveling companion in a panic:

"Pardon me, *rebeleben,* I don't mean to disturb you, but could you please tell me what time it is? I don't have a watch."

The old Jew stops his reading, raises his head, looks thoughtfully at length at the young man, and, after a long silence, tells him very calmly:

"No."

"You don't know the time? What about the watch in your pocket?"

"I do know the time, but I won't tell it to you."

The young man is flabbergasted.

"You could but. . ."

"Yes. No."

"You are refusing to tell me the time even though you know it?"

"Yes."

The young man is beside himself. He looks at the landscape, then at the rabbi.

"I was supposed to change trains at Szolnok to go to Kecskemet. There is only one train per day. I can't miss it . . . That's why I took the liberty . . . But really, this is incredible . . ."

"Certainly."

"So now you have to help me and tell me the time. I'm afraid of missing my train. I have never been in these parts. I am from . . . You can't, you have no right to . . ."

"I don't want to give you this information."

"Why, I never . . . ! I've never heard anything like this! I let you study without saying a word for hours. And then, driven by necessity, I address you politely and I ask you a banal question, but an essential, existential one for me. I don't have the money to spend the night at the hotel in Szolnok, where I don't know anyone. This connecting train is thus crucial for me. And yet I'm not asking you for money; I'm not asking for your time, or your care, or your advice, or your attention, nothing like that. I'm only asking you for some simple information that any man, regardless of whom he might be, should give to anyone, even if we were not both Jews. But moreover we are. And moreover you are a rabbi, a holy man. It's thus your duty to help your fellow Jew."

The young man stands up; he gets angry. His face turns red. His sparse, frizzy beard quivers with excitement; he splutters as he is speaking and keeps on pushing back his hat over his abundant hair.

"I understand," answers his companion, "but I won't tell you anything anyway. And now if you will allow me . . ."

And he gets back to his book. The young man sighs and, desperate, turns silent. He can see the situation is hopeless. Then after a long silence:

"Pardon me again. I am not asking you anymore for the time; I've given up on that. But at least please explain to me the reason for your refusal. Do I seem to you so unlikable, repulsive? Is my breath so bad that you want to keep at a distance and not communicate with me? Have I unknowingly offended you in some way? Do you happen to know me and are so angry at me that you refuse something that is not even a mitzvah but a simple common courtesy?"

"It's nothing like that."

The rabbi leans back comfortably on his seat, stretches his legs, and yawns.

"Since you insist, I will tell you. I know perfectly well what time it is. I've had a specific reason to make this trip once a month for many years. I know it practically by heart. With my eyes closed, just from the noise of the wheels at certain places on the tracks I could tell you the name of the hamlet we have just passed and the time, almost down to the second, without even looking at my watch. Today we are terribly late. We should have been at Kéthalompuszta now but we're not even at Nagybotványtanya. But the names of these villages don't mean anything to you. It's just to tell you that you have already missed your connection at Szolnok."

The *yeshiva-bocher* again jumps up from his seat.

"Calm yourself. You can't make the train go any faster and, at any rate, the train for Kecskemet didn't wait for you. If I had told you this earlier, you would have started to utter *oyweh tsores,* sighs, and groans, and you would have gotten yourself so upset. I then would have had to calm you, to ask you the reason and destination of your trip so as to explain to you that your late arrival is not important, to console you, to offer you my hospitality at Szolnok for the night. You, well brought up and polite, you would have seen reason and calmed yourself, you would have refused, remembering suddenly that you have some distant cousins at Szolnok, or even the *yeshiva* where you could have slept. I would have had to insist; I am a rabbi, a holy man according to you, supposed to help, and I would have tried to change the subject of the conversation, thinking that we would have plenty of time to decide where you would sleep once we arrived at Szolnok. We would have thus started to chat, we would have had a discussion, and I would have discovered that you are well educated, knowledgeable in both the Talmud and modern sciences as well as in modern literature"—the young man opens his mouth to protest, we don't know from or against what, but the old man doesn't let him speak.

"I continue. So one thing leading to another, we would have made friends, you would have told me your family circumstances, we would have discovered common acquaintances, perhaps even common relatives, you would have forgotten your troubles, and when arriving at Szolnok and getting off the train, you would have been filled with joy and admiration upon making the acquaintance of my daughter, who always waits for me at the train station. My daughter is extremely beautiful; everyone wants to court her, and there's no dearth of marriage requests. She must be three or four years younger than you; how old are you?"

"Twenty-four years."

"I was wrong, she's only eighteen. No matter, or rather even better. You would have fallen instantly in love with her, at first sight, and you would have not only forgotten the train for Kecskemet, the problematical *yeshiva*, and the improbable cousins, but you would have been filled with only one desire: to spend the evening and night at our home. That's the way love works. It's the greatest power in the world, after that of the Eternal God, may He be blessed. And that's the way it should be. Or, if you prefer, it is through love that God gives meaning to our lives. Anyway, I have believed for a long time that the Divine and love are the same thing. But that's not the point here. To speak to my daughter, to hold yourself at a respectful distance from her, would have meant supreme happiness to you. And since you are young, poor, but handsome of face and body, and well mannered, you would have impressed my daughter with your speeches, your poetical compliments, your citations from the Psalms, from the Talmud, with your proverbs, your stories, your bragging, and she would have fallen in love with you, particularly since you came from elsewhere. You would have spent the evening talking to each other, you would have tried to come close to her, even to touch her dress (which she would have blushingly but glady let you do) while her mother left the room for a moment and I had fallen asleep in my chair. You would have played some music—she has the voice of an angel and plays the piano . . . You too I suppose? At the *yeshiva* . . .?"

"Violin," answers the numbed young man.

"Oh, you play the violin. Even better. You would have slept at our house, you would have recited your evening and morning prayers with me, I would have started to like you, and as for my daughter . . . it goes without saying. This way, for the price of the train ticket, you would have come more and more often to see Rebecca, until the day when . . ."

"But . . . ," the Talmudic student begins to say.

"Until the day when your parents would have made the trip to ask for her hand. Even without the intermediary of the matchmaker, directly, so much they would have been sure of their success, instructed by you."

"I am . . . ," tries to say the young man.

"An orphan—this doesn't change anything. Someone else would have come; it's a mere detail. But let us come back to the essential: Why did I refuse to answer your request for information? Because it's totally out of the question, young man."

And the old rabbi solemnly raises his finger, and his voice booms:

"It's out of the question that I give my daughter's hand to someone who doesn't even own a watch!"

THE GOOD CATCH

KOHN WAS THE MATCHMAKER in a small village in Po-
land. He was a *shadchen*. Well, to say "matchmaker in a village" is a
misnomer. A matchmaker can never stay in one place; his profession forces him to travel from village to village; he has to be constantly on the road to gather news as a thistle gathers dust, to glean
all the marvels, the horrors, the murders, the adulteries, the lottery
winnings, the shameful births, the happy deaths, the examples to
follow, and the examples to avoid. He has to draw the inventory of
eligible parties, of the couples to assemble, of the young and not so
young people he'll join for life.

Kohn practiced an important profession, the most important after that of God. He was arranging life.

You're going to ask me, "What about love?" You're going to
speak to me about leaning, attraction, choice, affinity, desire, elec-
tion, erection. You make me laugh! Marriages are made in heaven.
And the matchmaker knows what decisions are taken there. Because those who decide down here on the basis of "I-looooove
her/him and she/he loooooooves me," well, after ten years, or
rather after five years, . . . just ask them, they who gave themselves
flesh and heart to the other, ask them if their soul still desires min-

gling their body with the adverse, inverse, body after three years of common snoring-grunting under the same eiderdown.

Kohn says: those who don't choose each other have nothing to regret. It's possible that they'll come to curse me. But who can tell where I might be on that day?

Kohn says: let those with life experience, those who have lived, have become parents, have taught, let them decide. And the one whose job it is.

Kohn says: don't think that at age eighteen you know what you want, and that what you want is good for you. Couples are molded by marriage. They come together; the spouses take on each other's shapes. They become one, intrinsically inseparable.

So that's the *shadchen*. And from what does this personage, second only to God, live? He is given a part of the dowry. That's why he likes to fix up the poor with the rich. If he only united the rich among themselves, he would lose half his income.

One day, Kohn comes across Strauss, the poor shoemaker, in the street. He tells him as an aside, with an air of indifference:

"Strauss, I have a great match for you" (when they say "for you," that means "for your daughter, for your son").

Strauss is all ears. His daughter, his only child . . . What a burden. She is over thirty years old and has no husband.

"Please tell me, tell me!"

Kohn waits a long minute so as to heighten Strauss's eagerness.

"Let's go to your house—no need to entertain the whole village with our business."

Once comfortably installed in the parlor of the little house—Strauss is not rich, as I said—Kohn lets Strauss offer him a glass of vodka and latkes. Then not wanting to make the poor Strauss languish any longer, he hits him with:

"He's twenty-three years old, six feet tall, blond, blue eyes, speaks three languages, and has a high rank in the navy."

Strauss has trouble catching his breath. He empties two glasses of vodka before he is able to speak.

"Kohn, this must be a dream. And what faults does he have? Why wasn't this admiral engaged years ago?"

Kohn ignores the question and adds:

"I forgot to mention that his parents are immensely wealthy and he is an only son. He is not an admiral, but it's a family tradition for them to be officers, in the navy."

Strauss suppresses the urge to throw himself at Kohn's feet.

"Kohn, I beg you, arrange a meeting with his parents as fast as possible."

Kohn promises and leaves. As he opens the door he turns toward Strauss and tells him:

"He has a tiny flaw, nothing important. He isn't Jewish."

Strauss falls back on the arm of the chair, which breaks.

"What! A small flaw you say? Kohn, have you gone mad? It's totally impossible. To give my daughter to a *goy?* But I'd rather die, Kohn. It's even worse than my death. It's the death of my daughter that you propose, and you even joke about it. Aren't you ashamed?"

Kohn answers very calmly:

"You are the one who should be ashamed. It is said in the Talmud that your first duty is to insure the marriage of your offspring. A Jewish woman must marry and have children. It is written. And now that I bring you the best match you could ever dream of, you keep on sinning, you keep on not wanting to marry your unfortunate daughter who wishes it so dearly."

Strauss is not well versed in the skill of *pilpul*. He runs short of arguments.

"But to a *goy*, really!"

"Strauss, did you take a good look at your daughter Rebecca? Allow me to be frank, just between you and me. She is in her thirties; she is sickly, she squints and limps, is flat-butted and flat-chested . . . No, don't get up, don't be angry. I'm a matchmaker, I'm only doing my job, and you, you're the father, you have obligations. So, don't make trouble. I repeat, she has nothing to fill a man's hand—or his pockets for that matter, as you are as poor as Job, and you can't give her any dowry. You see, I am doing this out of friendship, because you won't be able to pay me."

"But the others, since they are wealthy, they'll pay you . . ."

"They'll give me nothing, since you don't want their son!"

Strauss puts his head between his hands.

"Kohn, you are torturing me."

He stands up, sways, paces round and round in the room, then suddenly, he stands up straight and declares:

"The answer is no! She will remain an old maid rather than abjure the faith of her ancestors!"

"As you wish," replies Kohn, who is outwardly relaxed but a maelstrom of agitation inside. "It's your life, your daughter. *Shalom.*"

And he leaves.

The *shadchen* is barely in the street when Strauss catches up with him.

"Don't go so fast. There's no hurry. Come back, have dinner with us, we can talk in peace."

"What do you want to talk about? You have made up your mind. You are a good Jew in keeping your daughter in the religion of her ancestors. You cause only a very little bit of her immense unhappiness and yours along with it; she will never know a man, she won't have children, you will never hold adorable grandkids on your lap; your Rebecca, your daughter, will become an old maid, irritable, grumpy, sad, she'll remain sickly, will even become very ill—and you, you who believe yourself to be a good Jew, you'll realize you're a bad Jew, because you are not respecting divine prescription. I would not blame you for absolutely wanting to give your daughter to a Jew if she were eighteen years old, if she were as beautiful as spring, as Perlmutter's daughter, for whom I found a magnificent match last month, and if your name were Rothschild. But none of this is important as long as you are happy with yourself."

Strauss goes crazy. He doesn't know what to do, how to respond, what decision to make. So, yes, he'll give his daughter to this young *goy* so suitable in other respects, and on the eve of this shameful wedding he'll go away, leave the village. He'll take to the road as a traveling shoemaker. But then who will take care of my poor wife, who is so often bedridden? Well, she'll just have to come on the road with me . . . Oh, no, I don't mean this, I am not going away. This is my village, my house, my work, the people here know me, my life is here.

They sit down to eat. Kohn fills his belly, eats and drinks, raises his glass to the health of the Strauss family more and more often. As Rebecca is serving the meal, Kohn keeps on giving meaningful glances to the father. To his chagrin this latter realizes the extent to which his daughter is unattractive. He has never looked at her the way a man looks at a woman; how could he have dared? She's his daughter. But now things are serious. He looks at her discreetly: everything Kohn said about her is true. And moreover she's over thirty years old. She'll never marry. And suddenly, almost miraculously, there is a possible husband. It's the first time, and certainly the last. He must agree. After all, who knows, perhaps he'll want to become Jewish?

"Say, Kohn, do you think this young *goy* would agree to convert to Judaism?"

"Frankly, Strauss, I don't think so. We could try to ask the question to his parents, but it seems to me to be difficult, not probable."

"But who are the parents?" asks Strauss.

"The king of England, and the young man is the Prince of Wales."

There's an astounded silence.

Strauss is dumbfounded, overcome. One of the biggest fortunes in the world. Of course, the Prince of Wales is an officer in the British navy. The greatest navy in the world. And England is the greatest naval power. Of course, in those circumstances . . .

"You know, Strauss," remarks Kohn, "that the English royal family claims to be descended from David? Did you know this? From King David, thus they are Jews."

Of course, in these circumstances. But really . . . David, that was a long time ago. And then . . . surely they don't eat kosher every day. Do they respect the Sabbath?

Kohn senses that the fish is biting. He keeps on going; this is not the time to let go. He gives it some slack, then pulls again, then more slack—he makes Strauss drunk, drowns him with words, with true and false arguments, as many as possible . . . all the science, the mastery of the matchmaker is revealed in moments like these. Like a fisherman. Like a toreador—but corridas are getting scarce in Poland in these years. Kohn exerts himself. He breaks into a sweat. It's now that he's truly working. He doesn't give Strauss time to catch his breath, or think. Then, when Kohn feels he has reached Strauss's psychological breaking point, a point when nothing more should be said, he suddenly turns silent.

The meal ends in silence. Kohn is exhausted. As for Strauss . . . The English royal family . . . that, he hadn't expected. He asks to think it over for the night, which Kohn gracefully grants him, but not more.

I won't describe to you Strauss's night. Hell in comparison to this night would be like a tour on a rowboat in a sunny lake in the shade of weeping willow trees. I won't describe this night, as you have all experienced similar ones, you who are pious and more attached to ancestral values than to reason or, even worse, to feelings. I'll only remind you of the terms of the equation: on the one side, the Prince of Wales, on the other, Jewish law. The choice is horrendous, and I don't wish it upon you, in spite of the nights of insomnia you've all spent pondering identical decisions.

But since we are speaking among ourselves, and we have a bit of time while Strauss tussles with himself, you might ask me, what does the hapless Mrs. Strauss think of all this? Strauss is a domestic tyrant, and his gentle and miserable wife has only the right to say yes and amen. And don't think for a moment that this is only appearance, that she organizes everything in the shadows, as so many of her sisters in fate are doing. No, she simply doesn't exist. But that's another story . . .

The next morning, or rather, at dawn, Strauss runs to the inn where Kohn stays when he is at the village. He runs to announce his decision to the matchmaker. It's yes! He does agree. His daughter's happiness has prevailed over his attachment to the faith. He wants to see the parents immediately, so that the deal can be concluded.

Where are they? In whose house are they staying? What if someone swipes his Prince of Wales? Kohn appears at the door of the inn as if he had been waiting for him.

"Kohn, my answer is yes. I can't tell you how hard this is on me, but my daughter's happiness comes first, even if it must be a bitter happiness. All right, since that's the only way, I'll accept the British royal family."

Kohn sits down on one of the steps that leads to the inn. He pulls out an enormous red and dirty handkerchief from his pocket, as if to wipe off the sweat from his brow caused by so much work, and says in a very low voice, with his eyes vacantly looking straight ahead:

"Whew! The most difficult is done. Now all I have to do is convince the king of England."

OPEN-FACE SANDWICH

IN THE TRANSYLVANIAN TOWN of Nagyvárad, there lived around the decade of the seventies of the century preceding our own (ours to be specific, the twentieth in the order of centuries, nicknamed the "joyous . . . ," that is, before the time comes to announce another one I foresee to be even more joyous, if that's possible), so in the nineteenth century there lived a very pious Hungarian Jew, respectful of the *mitzvahs*, the rules and the commandments, the laws and the Law. He was called Schönberger Izráel and was a pipe maker, a profession sufficiently lucrative, at this epoch and in this enchanted part of the bicephalous empire, to be able to raise twelve children born of the same mother, children who, in their turn, gave their father ninety-eight grandchildren. (It happens that this Schönberger Izráel was one of my ancestors, the grandfather of my paternal grandmother; and it is from the ghetto of this same good town of Nagyvárad—the one the poet Ady had called "the Paris on the shore of the Körös River" on account of the intellectual effervescence and the sweetness of life that reign there—that his countless descendants, barring a few isolated exceptions, were, one hundred years later, deported to Auschwitz.)

That is the time usually referred to as La Belle Epoque, which explains the resignation with which Izráel endured the ragging, the insults, and the various administrative and personal humiliations that were the daily lot of Belle Epoque Jews in happy countries. (At the time, Transylvania was a happy country. As to the location of this area, I will not insult you by telling you where it is. Bukovina, Ruthenia, Vojvodina, Pomerania . . . that's all you know, given the perfect knowledge Western Europeans have of the history and geography of the other Europe, the Eastern one.) Never did Izráel utter a complaint against the One who concluded an alliance with His people and led it into the country of Canaan but who twice allowed the destruction of the Temple, and created Egyptians, Romans, the Very Catholic Kings of Spain, Polish priests, Cossack hetmans, and Hungarian politicians. Izráel put up with insults, ignored humiliations, and forgave offenses because he understood from his earliest childhood that everything was good, was as it should be, and that the Holy One, blessed be He, could not have made a mistake. In his soul he wasn't humiliated, spittle soiled only his caftan, and every Friday evening he thanked the Almighty for His immeasurable kindness toward him.

In spite of this he worried. There was a sign that led him to wonder whether his heart was impure and whether he was truly fulfilling all the conditions required to be loved by his God, the Eternal One. This thought was becoming unbearable. While he could make all the injustices committed by human beings against him fit into his vision of the world, this divine sign profoundly troubled him. He didn't specifically know what it was that troubled him the most: the sign, unpleasant in itself, or the probable cause of this sign, the darkness of his soul. He felt this way because no divine error could be conceivable.

Every working day, around ten in the morning, Izráel took a break from his work. He poured himself a glass of red wine, cut a large piece of black bread, put goose fat and slices of raw onions over it, and sprinkled them with paprika (my mouth is watering as I am telling this). Each time, the piece of bread he had prepared fell from his otherwise skillful hands, and each time, it fell on the wrong side, the side with the goose fat facing the ground. What was the fault he might have committed and repressed, what was the low, shamefully forgotten deed, the wicked thought hidden even to himself that was thus reminded to him? In vain did he question, analyze, introspect, dig into, feel, scratch, look at, listen; in vain did he put his own self under scrutiny: he found nothing in the past or in the present with which to reproach himself, not in his actions, or in his thoughts, or in his words. Was God mocking him? Could that be possible? Was there a known precedent? And then, how did he come to deserve the distinction of divine mockery? The idea of accusing God of injustice was instantly extirpated from his heart as soon as it germinated. And yet . . . didn't Jonah rebel against the Lord? And Jeremiah? Ezekiel? Joshua! Didn't Moses himself contradict his Creator? True—but Abraham was willing to sacrifice his son rather than doubt divine justice—the only justice.

Izráel wanted to know. What horrible sin was being punished with this unbearable punishment? And if the fall of the bread was not a punishment, what did this sign announce? And if it was not a sign, what was it exactly? The paprika started to burn his palate, the onion made his eyes cry, the grease became rancid and the bread a suffocating paste. Izráel couldn't stand this suffering and, even though he was but a simple maker of pipes who earned his daily bread from the labor of his hands, his mind couldn't stop thinking; his thoughts kept on popping up, kept on straddling each other, multiplying, filling the dark side of his life. The time had come to find the light, regardless of the price. He went to see the rabbi of his community, whom he venerated and held in esteem.

"Rebbe," he told him, "you know me: I work, I study, I pray. I do my best to be a just man. Why doesn't God love me?"

"He does love you," answered the rabbi. "Your house is prosperous. You have twelve living children, which is exceptional, a rare gift of God to those He favors. Your grandchildren are already numerous; they'll multiply. Just by yourselves, you Schönbergers are almost going to become a nation. Your wife Rachele is a good mother, a pious woman who takes care of everything and of you too. What can be missing?"

"The peace of soul that only God's love can give. Like you, like everybody, but probably a bit more, I love black bread with goose fat, paprika, and onions: well, the slice of bread, when it slips through my fingers, always falls on the greased side. Why?"

The rabbi came to the conclusion that the question was worth asking and meditating over.

"Come back tomorrow," he told Izráel.

When this one went back to see the rabbi the next day, that one received him with open hostility.

"I spent the whole night thinking. I am not learned enough. I consulted the Torah, the Talmud, and even the Zohar, and I didn't find the answer to your question. But I am sure that you are a great sinner, and that you must continue your quest in order to finally get to know yourself and find out what is the fault for which you are punished. Hurry up—I am afraid that you might contaminate the whole of the community. Go quickly. Confide in the rabbi of Kolozsvár, who is very wise."

The pipe maker had never taken a trip, and, at any rate, he hated the idea of it with the whole of his being. He hated any change, any move, any lack of order, and he particularly abhorred uncertainty. He decided to follow his rabbi's advice, not because he believed him about his sins but because this latter had not been able to help him. He thus had to look elsewhere. He had his cart hitched, said good-bye to his wife, to those of his children still living at home, his servants, workers, and neighbors, and without revealing the goal and motive for his journey, he left for Kolozsvár, accompanied for what seemed a very long time by his wife's lamentations and his children's crying.

The rabbi kept him waiting. When Izráel was finally let into the darkened office, where the family in all likelihood was also taking its meals, as it was permeated with the strong smell of cabbage, he became frightened. He realized only at that moment the implication of what he was doing. He understood suddenly that what was at stake was nothing less than the tranquility of his mind for the remainder of his life—and long afterward. He was going to learn, because he had to know, the Reasons, the Causes, and the Origin. The definitive Explanation:

For him,

For his family,

For his whole people.

What are we guilty of? Why have we continually been punished since the destruction of the Temple?

The rabbi listened and asked him to come back in three days. It was three days lost for Izráel's shop and family, but what were three days when it came to eternal inner peace? He was ready to pay this price, and even much more.

The rabbi of Kolozsvár was an ignorant man. After making Izráel pay him a large sum of money, he told him bluntly that his case was utterly devoid of interest, that the slice of bread surely fell at times on the right side and at others on the wrong side, just as the sun sometimes shone and sometimes hid behind the clouds, and that Izráel's negative mind, to say the least! was only conscious of the clouds without ever, in its blindness, noticing the sun, just as he didn't perceive the infinite goodness of the Eternal God. At any rate, to ask all those questions, to attempt to explain His Will was already a sin deserving of punishment—a punishment that was in the present case the fall of the slice of bread of which Izráel complained. The rabbi advised him to stop his arguments, his *pilpul,* to go back home, and to accept his bread falling the way the Lord wants it to fall.

Izráel decided to look for someone else who could dissipate the clouds of his mind and let the sun shine in all its brilliance. A *yeshiva-bocher* suggested he go to the wonder-rabbi of Szatmárnémeti.

"Only he, and he alone, besides the Lord, can help you."

Izráel, having forgotten he had a family, a shop, a life elsewhere, in the past, left for Szatmárnémeti. Yet the next day was *erev shabès,* the eve of the Sabbath, and he had never celebrated the Sabbath without his family. But he had lost them along the way, and it was a single man who tried to pray in the synagogue of Szat-márnémeti. The ceremony had barely begun when the roof of the synagogue opened up, a terrifying and milky light invaded every-thing, and Izráel was swallowed up and tossed in the air as if he were a wisp of straw by a dizzying tornado that forced him to close his eyes, made him hold his breath, and stopped his heart. This lasted for years.

And then, just as suddenly, he found himself back in his place in the synagogue, in the midst of other Jews chanting and sway-ing, without his neighbors being aware of anything. He under-stood then that he was of no weight, no substance, no duration, no import, and that the supremely Good could appear to human eyes as just or unjust. Human beings were the playthings of the Eternal God; they were tossed about, blown about like dead leaves, at the mercy of the wind.

But man didn't deserve this. Not when he was pious and good, as he, Izráel, was.

"Eternal God, One and Only God, look upon me. I honor You as You ordered us to do. You cannot treat me this way. Your arbitrari-ness . . ."

He felt the solid ground of faith slip under his feet, which was more terrifying than to be lifted up in the air. He felt the mad wind of revolt rising in his topsy-turvy head.

As soon as the Sabbath was over, he rushed to the wonder-rabbi. He had to wait his turn for days and days in the courtyard, in the midst of a crowd of numerous, noisy, and joyous *hassidim*. Seated, standing, lying down, he was indifferent to the others, to their dances, their songs, to the hours, the minutes, to his body.

The renown of the wonder-rabbi of Szatmárnémeti had spread beyond the borders of Transylvania. Jews and Christians came to consult him from Budapest, from Bucharest, from Czernowitz, from Kichinev, from Vienna, and from Warsaw. (His disciples claimed they even came from Paris, even London . . .) He reestab-lished peace among enemies, healed the sick, chased away *dibbouks* from the minds and bodies they possessed, and he made sterile women fertile.

He was an enormous, unkempt, old man seated in a colossal armchair covered with threadbare red velvet.

"I've heard about you," he told Izráel.

"But, *rebelebe*, what you don't know is that while I was praying, I was lifted up in the air . . ."

The rabbi interrupted him with a thunderous voice.

"How old are you?"

Schönberger Izráel told him.

"Do you love the wife who gave you twelve living children?"

The pipe maker remembered his wife, his children, his town, his street, which had all been lost in a distant and improbable past. It was as if he had been traveling forever in his cart, alone. With no respite.

The rabbi's voice brought him back to reality:

"Did you visit foreign countries in the past?"

Not only had Izráel never left Nagyvárad, but neither had his ancestors, as far back as he knew. They were sedentary and very pious Jews: craftsmen, grape growers, shopkeepers . . .

"How can you call sedentary our nomadic people, driven from country to country ever since leaving Israel? Our home is the road . . . But that's not the point. You either don't know or don't want to know. I believe you don't know; you know very little, it seems to me . . . Your father, what was his occupation? How old was he when he died? How many brothers and sisters do you have? What are they doing? Where are they living? And your grown children, what are their occupations?"

When the rabbi was through asking these questions and many others, all completely useless and without relation to Izráel's falling slice of bread, he closed his eyes and remained as if he were dead. Izráel wished he could unload the boiling anger of his burning heart, give vent to all of the thoughts of his mind drowning in a sea of revolt: "God is not just. He lifted me up in the air just as He made my bread fall to the ground. He is toying with me. It's useless for me to love Him, since He doesn't love me, and I don't care if I am damned, since I am already damned on earth."

But he did not dare speak.

After a long, immobile silence, the rabbi opened his enormous eyes, fixed them on Izráel, and stood up with all his height, leaning with both hands on the table, which groaned.

"All is well," he said. "The Eternal Tsebahot our God, may His Name be blessed, is just. Obviously. *Ob-vi-ous-ly*. He never makes a mistake, you hear, never. Everything happens always, everywhere, as He foresaw for all eternity. And He does love you, *ob-vi-ous-ly*. Even though your brain is confused, and is getting more and more confused by the minute, and you dare have guilty thoughts, your heart is pure. The piece of bread that falls is not the sign of His anger. You are not an evil man, just a stupid one. Your piece of bread always falls the way it's supposed to fall, when it's supposed to fall, and where it's supposed to fall.

"But it's you, *meshüge,* imbecile, who are spreading the grease on the wrong side.

"*Shalom.*"

THE BLONDE

THE YESHIVA-BOCHER IS DEAD; he was barely eighteen. He was scrawny, haggard, diaphanous from birth; already as a child his posture was bad, his stomach stuck out, his back was rounded, as if bent under the weight of the future. His parents, his family, but also the whole shtetl thought that only studies would suit him because the speed of his intelligence, the way he could think, his memory, his ability to abstract were as strong as his physical frame was weak. He liked to daydream, was secretive, withdrawn, taciturn. People predicted a brilliant career as a rabbi for him. And yet, all his strength, all his abilities proved not enough; they did not succeed in enabling the *yeshiva-bocher*'s body to cross the barrier of time.

While his family was still crying, while the whole unhappy community was very sad to have lost the one who might have become its pride (and perhaps its wealth)—perhaps a wonder-rabbi more famous than the one of Tarnopol, more learned than the one of Berditchev, more astonishing than the one of Lemberg—the lad was in the process of sliding down screaming on the dizzying drop to Hell. His mother had just barely seated herself on the small stool, his father had not yet torn his clothes, when the terrified young man was already dragging himself through the stinking streets of Gehenna while awaiting his punishment.

All of a sudden he was gripped by a hellish terror. He was more than surprised; he was astounded, dumbfounded. There was his old teacher, the rabbi of his village, who had died recently. The young man venerated the rabbi—what was this saintly man doing among the damned? The old rabbi hadn't changed: he was bent forward, practically folded in two, and he was wearing the same black, threadbare, stained, darned caftan he wore in the village, the same worn-out boots; on his head was the same moth-eaten fur hat that everyone knew him by. His gray side curls, dirty, flaked with dandruff, curled up in front and behind his ears, and, in spite of the stench of the place, he smelled from afar of rancid tobacco just as he had on earth barely two weeks ago. He was walking slowly, with a labored, uncertain step through the suffocating vapors, while dragging his feet just as he used to in the mud and the refuse of the main street of his village. From time to time, he spat on the ground—if we can call "ground" the matter out of which the dia-bolical paths are made.

And, oh, surprise! Incredible, astounding, yes, unbelievable sur-prise! On his arm was a young beauty, a splendid woman, proud, with a straight posture, at least a head taller than he, blonde, her very long hair of gold and light falling on her round, bare shoulders. She was the *shikse* of all salacious fantasies. She was wearing a dress that showed off her perfect and provocative figure instead of hiding it. Her blue eyes, of an almost celestial blue, emitted gazes that were at once perverse and innocent, innocent-ignorant of the sin that the whole of her being, but particularly her inviting gaze, made one immediately yearn to commit. Her bearing, the lines of her neck, her throat, her hips, the sway of her walk, the young woman's every step, the least of her movements, were worth eternal damnation.

The young man immediately lowered his eyes, and he addressed the old man from a distance:

"But really, *rebele,* what is this? Is this how you are punished? Is this how your destiny is fulfilled? Is it with this most beautiful of women, this doe, this gazelle, this antelope, this mare [the young man was getting carried away], this dove, that you are suffering? You must be in Hell because of your sins, though I have trouble comprehending what they might have been. If you are here you must have deserved it. But then, where is your punishment? I see only gift, reward . . . You always taught us to avoid the temptations of the flesh, to never look at a woman, even to avoid their presence, to throw ourselves into books, into study. And you?! In such a company, and here, moreover? With this . . . this, oh God, forgive me, this . . .? who doesn't look like any of the women of our village, like any women I ever imagined in my lifetime [and he had imagined plenty of them, young girls, women, . . . every night, even during the day when he was pretending to read the Talmud]. And you, here, in Hell, with a creature of earthly dreams . . ."

And the old man, even while holding under his arm the shapely bare arm of his companion, raised his left index finger just as he used to do in the study room, and said with a serious but very sad voice:

"Don't be mistaken. It's not at all what you think. I am *her* punishment."

IN NEW YORK

IN THE OLDEN DAYS of old, young David was a poor apprentice tailor in a poor shtetl in Ukraine. He became fed up with pogroms, political uncertainty, oppression by the tsar and various lords—small ones, big ones, and even the Biggest One—fed up with the obscurantism of his coreligionists' limited minds, with their superstitions, their beliefs, their blind faithfulness to the holy writ, their closure to any progress, and he was exhausted by poverty, hardship, unmet needs, fear, worries. He thus decided to leave behind him: old Europe, his old parents, his many brothers and sisters, old books, the old rabbi of the old shtetl, the old neighboring town's whores, young and old, Jewish and non-Jewish alike, the study circle of the young Jewish socialist workers, misery, fear, obscurantism, pogroms (etc., see above), and all the rest we don't know and that David himself could only remember while still on the boat . . . he had thus, as you no doubt already figured out, decided to emigrate.

And where did a poor but strong Ukrainian Jewish apprentice tailor migrate at the beginning of our century?

Where did he seek his fortune? You'd never guess.

Amerika!

In New York.

David had a distant relative there, an Ashkenazi-style cousin, the adopted son of one of his mother's great aunts' second cousins— and his best childhood friend's father. This father went to get David at Ellis Island at the very moment when the cops were leading him back to the boat; he became his sponsor, paid the required fee, provided explanations and an invitation, took him to his home, put him up with his son, treated him like a son, fed him, and found him work in a men's clothing store. We are referring to this man of unusual kindness, of rare—rare!—generosity and disinterest . . . as "he" because we know nothing of him, not even his name. Did David remember it later on, in the course of his long, unhappy millionaire's life? Did he remember this humble relative of a relative, his buddy's father, and did he even remember his buddy? Or once his fortune was made, did he forget them, look down on them, chase them out of his mind? Do you really expect me to provide you with answers to these rhetorical questions? He swept them away, buried them forever. That's what we are made of, all of us (I, at any rate, and I suspect you too). We have to forge ahead. Kindness, gratefulness don't pay—and over there in America, which was open, completely open, to wealth, to the "entrepreneurial spirit," as selfishness, uncouthness, and uncontrolled meanness were then called in the country of unlimited possibilities, everything had to bring a return, and gratefulness did not yield any profit; it was a burden; it always is.

Because David did become a millionaire, like all the others—not all of them, but those we heard about, we who remained on this side of SUCCESS (in capital letters, just as NEMECSEK's name was spelled out at his death. He was the hero of *The Boys of Paul Street*, the most beautiful novel about adolescence ever written, and whose Hungarian author, Ferenc Molnár, made his fortune in America, in the cinema, just like the other millionaires. One of his novels is *Liliom*).

But to get there . . .

To get there David had to travel a long, hard road.

At the time he found work (or, rather, when work was found for him) in the *schmates* store,* his friend's father finally found the woman who could replace the one he had abandoned in Ukraine (In where? Ukraine? What's that? In *Europa?* You don't say!), and David had to give up his space. He first lived in a miserable room on Hester Street, then another, then another, and so forth.

He was twenty years old. He loved women, he was alone, he wanted some action. But "good" women don't allow their skirts to be messed with *just like that*—they have to be wed. You had to be serious, religious even, while the "easier" or, rather, simply the more sophisticated or freer women wanted gifts, nights on the town, escapades, avatars; they wanted to swirl in swirls, or at least wanted attention, deep conversations, intelligent discussion on fashionable topics, solicitude . . . You thus needed either money, or culture, or love. And David lacked all of those. He was earning just enough to ward off starvation—when he was earning anything. The store had closed down, and David had been without work for months. Then he found a new job—which he lost in turn . . . life, in other words, the normal routine of life, the struggle for survival in which only sharks and piranhas manage to surface.

But the lack of women drove him crazy. For months and months, at age twenty . . . and he saw nothing but women, beautiful and not so beautiful ones, young and old ones, inciting and incited ones . . ., well, what do you expect at twenty . . . didn't you too? I sure hope you did, at twenty, and even before and even later . . . The more he saw them, the more he looked, the more he looked, the more that's all he saw.

One evening, he could stand it no longer. It was a hot summer night; he decided to go try his luck in a neighborhood as hot as the night, the streetwalkers' neighborhood. Jewish hookers were too expensive, ten, fifteen dollars . . . five for Ukrainian compatriots, just for you, my pretty boy, only for you, but nothing less, forget it.

"Hey, *schnorrer,* you should have stayed studying in the *heder!* If

*Literally, "the rag store."— *Trans.*

you don't have a dime, don't waste our time. Go try your luck with the black women."

So he did. A little bit intimidated, quite terrified—not only had he never made love to a black woman, but never in all his life had he as much as touched a black woman's hand, not even her little finger. This was a whole other world, right smack in the other other world that the New World was. How to speak to them? And what about the rest . . . Oh Lord!

But the flesh, at age twenty . . . David's needle, needled by this latter (the above-mentioned flesh) feared no obstacles, and drove the proud owner (of the needle) toward the most alluring prey, this in spite of the unfamiliarity of their color, behavior, language, and dress.

Alas! The most beautiful ones were asking three dollars for their services, the less beautiful two (but everything else went downward along with the rate), and below one dollar there was nothing doing. He could only look, only fill his eyes, his desire. No discussion, no haggling, no negotiation—nothing doing. Absolutely nothing; this in spite of all David's efforts, for in the needled state in which he found himself he had rapidly found the courage to argue and negotiate.

David had only eighty cents in his pocket. From whom could he borrow the remaining twenty? Where could he steal them? Impossible. And the women were adamant.

"One whole dollar or you'll get nothing."

So he returned home, humiliated, like a beaten dog with his tail between his legs, back to his rooming house where he had to cross the dining room to get to his room.

His landlady, a young Irish woman, recently widowed, of modest means, of modest appearance (meaning: very ugly, with reddish hair, squinting eyes, and a wart on her upper lip), quickly, immediately, understood the situation. She had seen David go out; she too felt the pull of the night; she saw David return, and David was a handsome lad . . . she felt sorry for him.

One doesn't speak of those things.

We neither.

It happened the way it happens, quite "normally" (can you please explain this word to me), between a man who . . . and a woman who also . . . David, in a generous mood, even offered her his miserable eighty cents, which the landlady accepted as normally as can be.

Time passed, and David put money aside, and he changed jobs again, and his new boss, noticing the brightness and cleverness of his new employee, asked him to become a partner in his business, and David acquired the store and pushed his former boss out the door, and he left his room, his landlady, and the Lower East Side a long time ago, and started to really make money, and more and more money and then some, and he had women, lots and lots of women, and paid much more than a dollar or three dollars or even ten or fifteen dollars for them, and oh, yes! he bought many stores, and became partners with a friend of his who was a banker—and twenty-five years later, he was at the top of his glory, on the twenty-fifth story of a building on Twenty-fifth Street, in the cushy office of the executive president, chairman of the board of a solid-serious-honest bank/gang of seasoned thieves totally lacking in scruples.

He was not very happy, but then he never had been: neither in the shtetl in Ukraine, nor on Hester Street, nor elsewhere, nor later; and ever, but this is of no import to us, happiness is a gift of the gods (this very un-Jewish plural is there on purpose).

One day his secretary announces a persistent visitor.

"Sir [this isn't right; in America they would use the familiar "David"—even a secretary, even if she can be fired without notice at the end of the week], David," she thus says, "a middle-aged lady and a man are here to see you. They claim to know you personally . . . They keep on insisting, I told them you were busy . . ."

"What's their name?"

"O'Shaughnessy."

"Let them in."

Of course it's too easy, the redheaded landlady with the wart on her upper lip. Accompanied by a young man, not very handsome, a bit mean-looking.

"What can I do for you?" asked David, recognizing her immediately but saying nothing.

"David, I mean Mr. Goldenberg, I don't know if you remember me . . . you used to . . . live in my house, a long time ago, twenty-five years ago . . . you were very young, very poor . . . and . . ."

There is silence, a silence that was painful for all concerned. She wants money, obviously. David is debating whether to give her any, and if yes, how much, in cash, does he have enough in his pocket, or in a check, but then he'll have to give a lot more, he should interrupt her, go out quickly, talk to his secretary about it so as not to lose time, and then speedily get rid of them . . .

But suddenly, in the midst of his thinking, she is still speaking. David hadn't been listening to her, but he now hears:

"And he's our son. I would like to introduce him to you."

Dumbfounded, David looks at him, this time carefully. He looks like him, but uglier! Oh God!

At that point a scream comes out of the young man's mouth, a scream of revolt, of horrible surprise:

"*Mom,* but he's a Jew! But then I . . ."

David doesn't let him finish. He sees red. He jumps up from behind his desk and stands face-to-face with the ungracious young man, looks him straight in the eye and yells:

"You miserable nitwit of a goy! Do you realize that if I had had twenty cents more you would have been black!"

IN SECRET, IN
THE DARK

ONE EVENING DURING THE 1950S, contrary to their
usual practice, Mr. and Mrs. Loewinger went out to dinner at their
friends' house and left their two children alone at home. They just
asked the neighbor who had a key to check on them before she went
to bed to make sure all was well, and they also told the concierge
they would be away. It was in Paris, in the Jewish neighborhood
of the Marais, that is, "the Swamp," the alternately blessed and
cursed neighborhood of the Saint Paul subway station. At that time,
leaving children alone was safe and no cause for worry. Public safety
was excellent, incomparably better than it had been in the seven-
teenth century, when no bourgeois from this neighborhood would
dare venture out unaccompanied, when one Parisian out of ten was
homeless. The Loewingers were in the habit of asking the daughter
of the baker on the corner of rue de Sevigné and rue des Francs-
Bourgeois to babysit and give the children their dinner. This was a
fairly rare occurrence. The Loewingers seldom went out in the
evening. During the day they worked—that was all they knew to
do—and evenings, after dinner, they read, balanced their check-
book, yelled a bit at each other, and then went to bed. This time,
the young girl had a previous engagement; she had promised to go

with her boyfriend to the Saint Paul movie theater where Marilyn Monroe was playing in *Bus Stop* and, quite understandably, she wasn't going to miss it and him for anything in the world.

We don't know why, but Mr. Loewinger insisted that it was time to experiment, to leave the children alone that evening without supervision. There was a heated and lengthy discussion. Mrs. Loewinger started out by refusing outright. She'd rather stay home, she'd rather get on bad terms with the Blums, she'd rather, yes, she'd rather die. They didn't have a phone, how could they know if . . . But Mr. Loewinger, contrary to precedent, won out . . .

"These children must get used to life. They can't be spoiled, watched, hide in their mother's skirt forever, etc. You let them go alone to school in spite of all those cars driven by maniacs, etc." (If only he knew, but he did know, the tortures his wife endured every day, morning and evening, when the children left and came back!) Why Mrs. Loewinger agreed to leave the children alone—we shall never know. We only know that dinner was hell for her, and also for her husband, and we know that, to the Blums' chagrin, they went home early, at ten-thirty PM, barely after wolfing down their dessert.

In this way the two children, Paula (ten years old) and Gabriel (eight years and four months old), found themselves alone in the evening for the first time in their lives, alone in the nocturnal, a bit frightening, empty apartment, empty of parents. Empty of the busy, noisy, odorous, and agitated life their parents created around them. It was a new, strange sensation. There were none of those constant problems adults are permanently secreting and for which they only succeed in coming up with solutions at the cost of reflection, discussions, arguments, lengthy silences, slammed doors, and false starts.

They certainly were not going to go to bed. It was much too early and the occasion was much too rare. It is then that Paula asked the traditional question to her brother:

"What shall we do?"

A new game.

"Let's play daddy and mommy."

This was not all new, on the contrary. It was the most worn-out game, but also the favorite, the most fun, one in which new things could be tried all the time and the daily contributions of life added. And yet, this time, Paula wanted to try a new variant. The night one. What do the parents do at night, when the children are asleep? At her age, she was a bundle of curiosity, worries, suppositions, half-knowledge, fear, presentiments. This game, they had never played it before. She never dared to.

"Come, follow me. The parents are still up. We are them. We first make the tour of the apartment. Yes, it's okay, you can turn the lights on if you're scared, but afterward we have to turn them off. You may hold my hand if you want. Is the gas turned off, at the main switch under the counter? Is the water heater set right? Was the pan that collects the water seeping from the pipe in the bathroom emptied? Are all the windows closed, even in the pantry? How about all the faucets? And the refrigerator door? And is the door locked with the dead bolt? I know they're not home, we're just pretending. Don't worry, we're not going to lock it. Come, Gabriel. Let's listen at the children's door. Are they asleep? Good. Let's crack the door a bit so we can see them. Shush! Don't make any noise. They're sleeping like angels."

"Is this what they say when they look at us?"

"Yes, haven't you ever heard them?"

"Never, I'm always asleep when they come."

"How do you know?"

"I don't know."

"Good. They're asleep. Now we can go to sleep ourselves. It's getting late. It's not true, it's just make believe. Come on, let's go brush our teeth."

"Say, can we just make believe?"

"Of course."

They say " brush brush," then they pretend to spit. Paula hesitates a moment as to whether she should pretend to take her makeup off, but she gives up on that. Then they both hesitate before deciding whether the parents go weewee before going to bed. They decide the answer must be yes. But Paula feels the game escaping them, and she brings her brother back onto less slippery ground. She thus orders a quick, straightforward weewee, and they enter into their parents' bedroom. This is dangerous. What if the parents come back! But it's still early; they have just left.

"Close the door so the children won't see us if they wake up and leave their room to go weewee. Okay. Now we get undressed."

"But one night, when the door wasn't closed all the way, I saw daddy undress mommy."

"Yes, I know. But this evening we won't do it that way because it's not much fun and it's very complicated and tiring. Let's both of us undress by ourselves. Fold your clothes neatly on the chair, like Papa does. Like this, I'll show you. You, you put your jammies on and I my nightgown. And then we get in the bed."

"No! I'm scared. In their bed, by ourselves? Without them? What if they come back?"

"If they come back, we'll tell them we were too scared and that's why we got into their bed. They'll believe this, for sure. It will even make them happy."

"All right."

The two children put on their parents' nightclothes. They look at each other, bursting with laughter. Gabriel's legs reach only to the knees of the pajamas, which anyway fall to the ground and the little boy has to hold them up; Paula could have made a sleeping bag with her mother's nightgown. But they keep them on, and laughing, terrified, and overexcited, they slip into the enormous parental double bed, under the enormous duvet, a duvet like they used to have "over there," in those distant and mysterious countries, at once hated and beloved, of which the parents speak so often with their friends, countries all at once extraordinary and frightening where the children have never been.

"What do we do now?"

"We listen for a while to make sure the children are asleep."

"Why?"

"So they won't hear us and won't wake up . . ."

"Oh, because the grown-ups, the parents do what now? They are making noises?"

"We are the parents."

"I know. I meant, what do we do next?"

Paula puts her arm under the head of her kid brother.

"Come close to me, like a grown-up. Put your head on my shoulder. At night, when no one can hear them and the children are fast asleep, the parents shut off the lights, they take off their jammies, they hold each other tight and, very softly, they speak Yiddish."

BREAKDOWN

[I]

THIS IS AN AMERICAN STORY. Another one! You're
going to accuse me of being obsessed with America. Me? No way.
But you, yes, like everybody. The supreme dream—and for Jews
of this century (as well as for the Irish, Armenians, Bogodshnians,
and so many others . . . except for black slaves imported against
their hearts' and bodies' wishes) it was the Cape of Good Hope. A
country without Cossacks. In Jewish stories, it's the country of
success.

Myriam Gordon, a young Jewish woman, a New Yorker with
an uneventful life—what? Not possible; let me rephrase: a life with
no more events than those of other mortals, meaning one filled with
human events—a professional woman is driving her Volvo (the intellectual's car) through the desert. It doesn't matter which one:
they have so many of them over there . . . Just as they have lots of
everything else. Americans have everything. Myriam has come here
on purpose. Tired of New York, of stress, of the times, of success, of
all that anxiety, tired of tiredness, she is fleeing. She is running away
from herself. Myriam likes the desert, the heat that she doesn't feel

in the air-conditioned car (the intellectual's car) but that can be seen in the vibration of the air, the solitude of the road, the wide-open spaces—like hope. Without limits, without the obstacle of others, she's alone and all-powerful.

She is speeding into the evening light. She loves speed, and her car is responsive to the slightest of her movements, of her thoughts. She drives faster and faster—why not? An intellectual's car, it's made to go, to go fast, that is. The only thing Myriam knows about the car is the gas pedal. That's all she needs. Her cars are always in perfect shape; she gets a new one every year. The road is clear. From time to time a sign, a phone booth—otherwise nothing.

She keeps on going, full speed. Then all of a sudden the gas pedal seems to not work; Myriam floors it, but the Volvo keeps on slowing down. The engine ceases to respond: without noise, without complications, without hysteria, without hiccups, without side jumps, without slamming doors, tears, false exits, without "I'm-leaving-forever-no-I-am-begging-you-to-stay"s; the engine simply, naturally, stops functioning.

Myriam stops at the side of the road and tries to start the car again. Nothing. It won't start. The key turns, there's the usual noise of a willing battery, but the engine is not willing, that is, the engine or something else. Who knows? Not Myriam in any case. As we've said, she knows nothing about cars. Nothing about human beings either: she has been going to a *shrink* for years to try to understand herself thanks to psychoanalysis. Myriam tries again. In vain.

What to do? Night is falling, there's no car in sight, none of these monster trucks that have always terrified and fascinated Myriam. Should she wait for a car with someone who could fix the problem or at least drive her to a gas station or to a phone? Hmm . . . To fix the car . . . as if men could be expected to know how to fix cars. A guy might pretend, might look under the hood and vaguely pretend to do something, perhaps even definitely break the whole thing. He would just use this as a pretext to try to pick her up. Should she hitchhike? That's dangerous. Myriam is a young and pretty person, better not to take a chance. Alone, in the middle of the desert, someone could get the wrong idea. Particularly truckers. But right now it's Myriam who is full of ideas. And anyway, why truckers?— as if a dentist could be trusted to control himself! Newspapers are filled with stories of rapes committed by bank clerks—even by cops. Myriam feels like saying, "particularly by cops." She hates them. In spite of this, she would be happy to see a highway patrol car stop at precisely that moment.

But nothing, no dentist, no cop, no trucker. Not a single *serial rapist* banker. No one. There's only the sun disappearing behind a dream horizon, the wind raising sand skirts and rolling tumbleweeds around. This seems tender, happy. It's not. Myriam has chosen the wrong desert. She should have picked a less desertic one, since there are so many around. One with McDonalds, Holiday Inns, Barnes & Nobles, highway patrols, a tamed desert. This one is too real. It's a deserted desert.

Myriam is very frightened. Very, but no matter; she has to act because in a few minutes the night will swallow up all this emptiness. She tries to start her engine one more time, now that it's cooled off. But the engine is asleep. There's no hope. It requires other means than those Myriam knows, more expert hands to wake it up. Myriam decides to walk. This solution seems reasonable to her. If a car should show up in any direction, she could always get a ride. That is, if she decides to, if the driver looks safe. She might also come across a pay phone. She believes there might be one every two miles. It's a long way, but she is young and in good shape. And maybe there's one nearby. That would be the best solution. She locks up all the doors, takes her purse with her money, her driver's license, her credit cards, and begins to walk on the road.

And luck smiles upon her: half an hour later, at a crossroad (roads that cross in the desert to go from nowhere to nowhere to elsewhere), a real phone booth, a little shelter against what? It never rains, in this desert. At the other end of the line, there's help. The number of a mechanic and a tow truck.

"Lady, wait for me at the phone booth. I'll pick you up there."

And it was done. The tow truck operator, with his wonder supertruck equipped like an operating room with everything an ailing car could dream of, arrived half an hour later. This desert did have secrets: a gas station only half an hour, that is, forty miles, away.

And already they're in front of the Volvo calmly and mysteriously enveloped in its taciturn refusal. Even the powerful lights of the tow truck don't succeed in waking it up; they search it, though. The mechanic takes the key and tries to get it started. He is met with only obstinate silence. Then he opens the hood, extracts from the clinical entrails of his tow truck a large hammer, contemplates it at length and suddenly gives a hard blow with it to the engine.

"Sit at the wheel, and turn the key," he tells Myriam.

She does, and wonder of wonders, the engine purrs, as happily as it used to in the distant good old days two hours ago. Myriam barely touches the gas pedal and the engine responds, all excited.

She is relieved, happy. She feels she has come back from far away. So that was all . . . a hammer blow was all that was needed . . .

Myriam is secretly disappointed. It's no longer possible to lose oneself. It's no longer possible to be alone. Danger no longer exists, nor the possibility of adventure. You cannot test yourself. Anguish can only be existential now.

Thanks, thanks again. How much do I owe you? She turns, beaming, toward the mechanic.

"Five hundred and fifty-two dollars, lady."

There is an awkward silence. Has she heard right? It's an enormous amount. And why this ridiculous number? She doesn't dare ask the mechanic to repeat it. He notices her embarrassment and politely repeats:

"Five hundred and fifty-two dollars."

Myriam is astounded.

"Five hundred and fifty-two bucks for a hammer blow?"

"No, I charge fifty dollars for travel—that's forty miles one way, forty the other. The hammer blow only costs you two dollars. But the knowledge of where to give it, that stands for fifteen years of ex-

perience, daily work, fatigue, pain. The charge for this is five hundred dollars."

ψ ψ ψ

[11]   *In memory of Melsene*

There is a divine version of this story. I say "divine" advisedly. A
story in which Myriam, instead of stupidly driving her stupid car in
the desert, wants to go to a superchic New York cocktail party and
cannot find a hat to match her Dior *new-look* dress. She just has
time to run to the Dior boutique to buy a hat—but she can't find
one that pleases her. By an incredible chance the Master himself is
there—incognito?—incognito to Myriam, at any rate. He takes a
piece of cloth, twirls and twirls it, shapes it, and puts it on top of
Myriam's brand-new shiny hairdo, pats it, arranges it, pulls it here,
flattens it there and . . . a delighted Myriam exclaims:

"Yes, that perfect! This hat is perfect on me. It's exactly what I
was looking for! I'll take it, I'll keep it on my head. What do I owe
you?

Dior asks for two thousand dollars.

Myriam's stupefaction:

"But really . . . So much for a bit of cloth?"

Christian Dior takes the piece of cloth, carefully folds the now
limp material that had been a hat a moment earlier, personally puts
it in a bag marked with the famous "CD," and gives it to a green and
dumbfounded Myriam while telling her pleasantly:

"It's free, madam, with the compliments of the house."

Divine, I already told you. Because, besides love, only creation is
divine (and so is laughter).

THE DREAM

MADAME LALOUCHE, a Parisian Sephardic Jew, is dreaming. She's happy to be dreaming—it's been so long! Ever since her
husband—what husband? that total jerk, that bastard, he'll have
to pay for what he did, you'll see, I'll give it back to him, with interest!—ever since Maurice, that crook, that thief, that lying cheat, left
with that slut, that whore, that washed-out blonde and her humon-
gous tits, that miss hoity-toity-bullet-boobs-bitch who tried to look
like a fifties star and dared pretend to be my friend, I must have been
a blind, stupid, idiot not to have seen their goings-on already five
years ago at Club Med; they said they had the same tastes, the same
leeeeeeanings, ha! I'd gouge your left eye out with your leanings! It
was only because of her tits and because she's blonde, you nitwit,
because you couldn't see she's a fake blonde, totally fake, on the pil-
low, in bed, when you were close, you saw nothing, the roots, idiot,
it's not glasses you need, it's a dog, you pig!

Madame Lalouche has stopped dreaming since Maurice Lalouche abandoned her; she stopped dreaming because she stopped
sleeping. Sleeping pills don't help; nothing helps.

This night though, God knows why, she is dreaming. She felt the
beginning of the dream; she even said to herself, "Interesting, I'm

dreaming" (can we dream of ourselves dreaming?). It was sweet, peaceful. Somewhere warm, it felt good. She was naked or almost? Was she wearing her short nightie, the pink one with laces on its front, that Maurice loved so much, and thus she too? She wasn't to know. She is walking, in a forest, very warm, humid, her skin sticky from sweat; it's a tropical country, it must be like this, the tropical forest. There's daylight but you see only trees, vines, thick and heavy leaves, a distant overcast sky, sounds that are unfamiliar to Suzy Lalouche. She isn't afraid, Madame Lalouche; she walks around aimlessly—but all of a sudden there's a noise, nearby, someone, an animal? The leaves rustle with heavy, quick footsteps. Now Suzy Lalouche becomes very scared, she would like to call out for help, but from whom? Alone in this forest; she knows no one in this country, far away from her home, from her husband, but where is he, that husband, now that she needs him? She flattens herself against an enormous tree trunk; its rough bark scratches her skin but she doesn't care. She is sweating, drenched; the humidity, her fear . . . her heart is pounding.

And then she suddenly sees him; there's a deafening yell as a huge hulk of a man, at least seven feet tall, his chest covered with hair, hair sticking out of his head every which way, and with large, hairy feet, appears. He seems to be a sculpture of living flesh, his greenish skin shining as if oiled, muscles rippling under the hair. He's naked—that's evident, it catches Suzy's eye—he isn't even wearing a loin cloth; he's all naked, a vine around the hips, totally naked. Suzy just has time to catch a glimpse of his nakedness, his stature, and she starts running as fast as she can, breathlessly . . .

"Maurice," she pants, "Maurice, come" but there's no Maurice in this forest, there's only she, she alone in the whole world, alone with this beast-like man and his eyes burning under his square, jutting forehead, a true naked monster. She is running, oblivious of hurting her bare feet, usually so sensitive, she hears her own breathing sounding like a gigantic bellows, she hears her heart beat, she hears her fear, her solitude; she knows she is defenseless against this brute force that is going to overcome her. But she runs very fast, for a long time, an eternity; she keeps on running and she hears the sound of the man's steps closing in. She runs faster—she wouldn't have imagined she could have so much strength, perseverance, resistance.

But the hulk's footsteps come closer and already she can hear his breath and the guttural yells coming out of his throat, of his chest . . . Suzy's breasts are trembling, she feels them, so small, no longer damp but drenched, she tries to protect them from snapping branches, they're so fragile. Maurice used to say he loved them in spite of their smallness, he even said he loved them because they were so cute. This man will crush them . . .

Suzy is exhausted. She feels faint. No matter. She feels the breath of her pursuer on the nape of her neck, she is even surprised to not feel his hand on her shoulder. She is going to give up, let fate run its course . . .

Beside herself, out of breath, her legs turning into cotton, her chest burning with each breath, her skin covered with scratches, numbed, her head spinning, plunging, Suzy drops to the ground, flat on her back. She raises her head in an ultimate effort, turns toward the figure who is bending over her:

"What do you want of me?"

The man stands up very dignified and indignant. He takes a step backward and says in a wounded tone:

"Excuse me, ma'am, there appears to be a misunderstanding. Who's the one dreaming here, you or I?"

SEX

TWO PARISIAN JEWS, Friedländer and Bensimon, meet on a train. They have known each other for a long time; they are friends, close friends, very close. There's a noisy and long show of friendship, exclamations of joy from the classic repertoire—as if they hadn't seen each other since . . . in fact they had lunch together just a week ago (the variant, played often as well, is to not greet each other and to pretend to continue a conversation that was stopped ten days ago as if it had been interrupted only ten minutes earlier). There's a string of "Hey, buddy, how's it going?" and they slap each other on the back, on the stomach, and emit all sorts of yells and gestures and signs—this for a good long while. And then there's an awkward, embarrassed silence, unusual between them.

"You seem peaked," says Bensimon, after the deluge of disjointed gestures and joyful exclamations dies down.

"You're right," answers Friedländer, instead of bragging about his good health and happy mood as is customary in this sort of chance encounter.

"What's the trouble? Business? You need only say one word and you know I . . ."

"You're very kind, but that's not the problem. My business is going great—you did hear of the Szlagman sale; I talked to you about it . . ."

"Yes, I know of it: you made out great, it's a fantastic deal. So then, what's wrong?"

A heavy silence falls again. One can hear the clickity-clack of the wheels on the rails.

"It's hard to explain . . ."

Friedländer wants to talk about it. After all, Bensimon is one of his best friends. You don't get many of those in a lifetime. He has always given him good advice. Friedländer is hurting because of what happened this morning with his wife. Because it happened again. He has to talk about it with somebody. This has been going on for too long; he can't stand it anymore. A man is a man, and he's in his prime. This can't go on.

"I have problems with Sarah; this has been going on for some time . . . well, no need to talk about it."

Friedländer has suddenly become embarrassed. He isn't ready to expose such intimate matters. It's too, too . . .

"Excuse me, but I have to read an important document before we get to Orléans. I'll call you tomorrow and we can talk about it."

But Bensimon insists. They're friends—and then he senses his buddy wants to talk. And it's getting too interesting. He takes Friedländer by the arm of his leather jacket.

"Tell me everything. Me, with Rachel, I've seen everything, experienced everything. I know women. Don't worry. I've known your wife since . . . well, as long as you've known her. We met her at the same time, at your mother's *seder;* she came with her cousin, Sidney Cohen, you remember?"

A pause.

"She has a lover?"

"Not at all. It's not at all like that. On the contrary, I might say— how should I put it— on the contrary, and that's the problem."

Now Bensimon is confused. How can it be "on the contrary"? If she doesn't have a lover, it means she doesn't have one, so where's the problem? So there can't be a problem.

"I have to tell you, she doesn't like *it.*"

"What *it*?"

Friedländer is sweating blood. His people, the Ashkenazi *maaaales* of Eastern Europe, are bashful. They're not in the habit of discussing this sort of thing as Sephardi do . . . Feelings are kept inside, stored up; they are not exteriorized.

"*It, it,* you know, going to bed, sex, fucking!"

Bensimon is an expert. He explains everything. It must be that Friedländer goes about it the wrong way. Nowadays women, they're not like they used to be. They have their needs; they make demands. They feel they have a right to pleasure, they too—not just come to bed, babe, spread your legs and slam bang, the whole thing over in two measures, three movements . . . literally!"

"If you only saw Rachel and me! What a circus! Oops, it wouldn't be good if you saw us! We'd probably have to move . . ."

Friedländer doesn't believe he's going about it the wrong way. She simply doesn't like it, that's all, she doesn't want it, she doesn't care.

"And then, she doesn't do anything for it. And of course that turns me off too. It's an all-around total catastrophe. She's such a beautiful woman, but at home, she wears any old thing. She only dresses to go out, for others. I come home evenings and she is in the kitchen with her worn-out apron and her old sweater; when we go to bed, she puts on her ugly nightgown, as if we were in a mountain hut. It's so baggy, she must have a dozen of them; I only see her in those . . . She would turn off a regiment of hussars deprived of women for a whole three weeks of maneuvers in the middle of the Sahara, I'm telling you. She is a very good cook, I'll admit, though not as good as my mother—you remember, you must have had dinner with us at least a hundred times, that was something—but at least she is trying; the apartment is clean, orderly, even my mother admits it; she also takes good care of our children, their studies, there's no complaint there . . . but in bed, it's zero. I've talked to her about it, several times. I complained, but she doesn't even listen to me, she doesn't answer. I swear, I'm looking at every woman as if I were a madman; I want to do all of them, they must sense it, I must be emitting the scent of a beast in rut, even in the office, you know, I never let on, I'm very careful, but the women, they sense it, they must, women have a sixth sense for that sort of thing. I'm going crazy, I'm telling you, I'm only thirty-six years old, I'm not going to give up sex at my age . . . this will end up badly . . ."

Friedländer can't stop. The sluices have opened and finally he can talk about it. To himself as well.

"Someone should talk to her, should tell her. I was thinking of asking my mother, but I suspect Sarah might take it badly. And her women friends, I don't know them well enough."

"Okay, I'll talk to her," says Bensimon.

He finds this amusing, even exciting.

"Only if you want me to, of course."

Friedländer hesitates.

"What are you going to tell her? You must be tactful—she's a very sensitive woman, you know, you just can't be casual about it . . . like, say, with Suzy Levy. Do you remember her?"

"Do I remember Suzy Levy? You must be kidding. Who doesn't remember Suzy Levy? The Vincennes–La Défense subway line perhaps! That's the only thing that hasn't taken a turn over her. Stop already, I'm hurting from laughing."

And they slap the palms of each others' hands raised over their heads. Then Bensimon lowers his fist.

"Trust me, I know how to talk to women. Results are guaranteed."

They arrive at Fleury-lès-Aubrais. They were supposed to change trains to get to Orléans, but Bensimon pretends he needs to stay there. At Fleury-lès-Aubrais . . . really. He has some business to take care of at Fleury. So they say good-bye. Bensimon is impatient; he can't stand it any longer. He watches Friedländer leave before hurriedly pulling out his cell phone.

"Hello Sarah, it's Bob. How are you, hon. And the kids? Everything cool? Okay, okay—me too, pretty good, thanks, I can't complain. Listen, I just left Danny. To Orléans, I don't know. I'm here on business. He is complaining. He looks unhappy. Can I be frank with you? You and I, we've known each other practically forever, how many years? It was, no matter. Can I be frank? You won't get mad at me? It's for your own good. I don't want to meddle, but it's for the good of both of you. You should make an effort in bed. You see what I mean? You get my drift? A man is a man. The two of you are young. But yes, he's complaining. What, but I am his friend—with whom do you expect him to talk? Don't get mad, no, I'm not the whole world, I'm just Robert Bensimon, his friend. And also yours. But that's what he says, that you don't listen to him, you don't even answer him. He'll end up having an affair if you don't watch it. There's more to life than cooking and vacations and kids and all that. A man needs a woman, that's all. Watch it."

Sarah is dumbfounded. As if hit by a Mack truck. Daniel's gone mad, or what? He's telling their most intimate life to anybody? Did he tell about the other day, about this morning in detail?

"Okay Bob, I'm also going to tell you something. I have no desire to make love with Daniel, is that it? Is that what he told you? Let's talk plainly, or what? Or it's him who doesn't want me? It's my fault now? I don't turn him on, that's it? And you think that he turns me on when he gets home and, even before kissing me, asks if his mother has called, and when we go to sleep Daniel takes the phone to bed with him to call his mother? I'm going to tell you what the problem is: Daniel lives for his mother. Our vacations? In summer we spend them at his mother's house at Le Rayol-Canadel, in winter at her chalet at Tignes. And his mother of course is always with us. During every holiday—we spend all of them at her house. And Friday evenings, every Friday evening, she comes to have dinner with us, yes, yes, every Friday that God makes she is there, all over the place, frowning, criticizing my cooking and the rest, the kids' clothes and what have you. I don't even listen to her. I fall asleep in my armchair in the living room . . . at my age, as if I were a little old lady, and she talks, she talks. And your buddy, every day, he calls his mother before leaving for the office in the morning, and in the evening when he comes home, the first thing he does is get on the phone to call her again. I know, I already told you this, I'm repeating myself, this stresses me no end; you need to know since you are meddling in our life. No, I'm not angry, I'm just telling it like it is, that's all. And my daughter is called Bianca, like her grandmother ... need I say more? She is between us, at our table, in Daniel's head, and obviously even in our bed. So I, I have given up, I don't even try anymore. Oh, she's not mean, his mother; it's rather that Daniel is nuts. He hasn't succeeded in growing up."

But Bensimon doesn't give up this easily. He feels an obligation. He made a promise to his friend. He has a mission to accomplish. He swallows his anger, which is beginning to rise, stifles his desire to yell at Sarah, to simply yell at her, as well as his uneasiness about getting involved in this now that he isn't necessarily the good guy anymore, now that he can't play the role he had intended to. He swallows, and begs the beautiful and young Sarah to make an effort, you're such a cool chick, you know I liked you too, and how, but I stepped aside for my friend Daniel who, well, let's not go there, it's ancient history. He begs her to reconquer Daniel, to save her marriage that is drifting away. She should do what she can to play the game, to *be* a woman, a real one, a seductress; she should go all out, seduce him, put on your perfume when he comes home, wait for him in the living room with a glass of whiskey, and not always in the kitchen with your old apron, yes, he told me that too, and in bed, let yourself go, give yourself, unleash your passion, I am sure that it's your true nature, I don't need to tell you, you know better than anyone, at any rate better than I . . ."

Sarah becomes uncomfortable. Enough. She doesn't want to hear a stranger talk about this sort of thing with her, give her this sort of advice as if she were God knows what, a slut. As if he were a pimp giving advice to his hookers.

"Then, bye-bye, Bob, thanks, we'll talk later. Say hello to Rachel."

But something is bugging her. So Danny is complaining. He talks about it with others. He who is usually so discreet. This must mean there's really danger in the home. I really should do something. And Sarah suddenly makes a decision. The big game? I'll go for the big game.

While the children are in school she goes to the Bon Marché. Casually, as if she wears only this sort of lingerie, and has worn it forever, she buys herself the sexiest, most provocative lingerie she can find and moreover in the color that brings out her very white skin: black; tiny lace panties by Christian Dior—she hadn't known one could spend so much for a pair of panties—a garter belt, mesh stockings, a silk camisole, a black *deshabillé* with red lace. It all costs her a fortune and she goes home, almost running. There's just time to pick up the kids at school and drop them at her mother-in-law's with a vague pretext—and already she is lasciviously, suggestively reclining, holding herself up with one elbow, on the living room couch, leafing through a magazine, dressed—or rather undressed—to kill in her new purchases, surrounded by a vapor, a thick cloud of the most fashionable perfume, incredibly expensive, incredibly heady, bewitching, irresistible, and which comes in a tiny cut-crystal container with the name *Je te*.

She pretends to be absorbed when the key turns in the lock, but her heart is pounding. She is playing it big, is risking a lot. Where is this going to lead them? A new life is beginning for them, a life of love, of wildness; they will rediscover the pleasure of their bodies. Sarah is moved; she doesn't feel quite ready for this upheaval.

Friedländer comes in.

"What's going on? What's this small lamp—why don't you turn on the big one? Oh my God, what's happening? Why are you all dressed in black? Did something happen to Mom?"

THE ILLITERATE AND
THE NE'ER-DO-WELL

ROSENBERG has had two lives. The first, a fairly brief one, he lived as a *schnorrer-looser* without hope of becoming anything else. It's only logical: a *looser* is a loser. He's a loser forever. The Yiddish term *looser* defines a state of being, not a set of circumstances. If a loser were in the process of becoming a winner, he wouldn't be called "a loser." There was nothing that could lead one to believe that one day Rosenberg, the *schnorrer-looser* from the French province of Champagne, would transform himself into a fighter, a powerful businessman from Arizona, U.S.A. In fact, the seed was already there, well hidden, and was only awaiting the opportunity to germinate.

[I]

Rosenberg the *schnorrer* was living in Troyes, the city that had once been that of Rachi. I could tell you many an anecdote about the capital of Pantoukès, about its history, its glorious past; I could describe for you its sights, its public edifices, its gardens, its grottoes, the essential role Aubard's city played in the discovery of the circum-trapeze, its great men, Julin Dupin, Chrétien de Troyes, its famous women, Sorguenphore d'Oïllevet (née Tsoresse), Colbas de Coutia and her world-renowned charcuterie . . . I could cite the volume devoted to the fifteenth century of the *Histoire des Français des divers états* [History of the French belonging to various estates], by d'Amans-Alexis Monteil (Paris, 1830), giving an account of the debate held by representatives of the various estates of the town of Troyes, but this town remains for me that of Rachi.* He was a Jew of medieval Champagne who feared Hebrew would disappear,[†] who spoke Judeo-French (according to Moshé Catane)[‡] or, according to others, *champenois,* the language of Champagne, and he was one of the creators of the Jewish thought of his time. He is one of our greatest philosophers, the equal of Maimonides. He was a wine grower and lived from the sweat of his brow. In his letters he complains that he doesn't have enough time to study during the grape harvest—and he wrote commentaries on the Talmud in the eleventh century that we still read today. (In 1288, the whole of the large Jewish community of Troyes was destroyed: those who refused to convert were burned . . . as usual).

This, the past existence of this famous ancestor-compatriot, so respected and admired, didn't prevent young Rosenberg from starving, or almost, in Troyes.

---

*The reader is advised against looking up any of the sights within Troyes and the communities surrounding it in any travel guide, or worse, traveling to Troyes to attempt to find them. As their hilarious names sometimes indicate, they are wholly the fruit of the author's imagination, along with the mysterious Pantoukès and a number of the characters mentioned, except for Rachi, Chrétien de Troyes, Monteil's book, and the references pertaining to Rachi's life and works that follow. Biro has invented French-sounding multilingual punning names for some of the characters: "Sorguenphore" is made up of *Sorg,* meaning "worry" in German, and *phore,* from the Greek meaning "to bear." "Oïllevet" comes from the Yiddish *Oyweh!* and "Tsoresse" from the Yiddish for "misfortune." As for "Colbas de Coutia," it can be interpreted as "dog sausage" in Hungarian.—*Trans.*

[†]Sylvie Weil, *Les Vendanges de Rachi* (Paris: Flammarion, 2000); Simon Schwarzfuchs, *Rachi de Troyes* (Paris: Albin Michel, 1991).

[‡]Cited in Schwarzfuchs, *Rachi de Troyes.*

He wasn't a professional *schnorrer.* He lacked the necessary skills to practice this age-old profession. He did not beg, he did not systematically con his coreligionists into parting with their money, he did not speak every language, he didn't have the traditional arrogance and chutzpah. And he was still too young. Rosenberg lacked neither intelligence nor resourcefulness, nor daring—it was rather that luck had not been on his side, not yet. Besides this, his body was in poor shape: skinny, puny, shortsighted, he looked like the stereotypical Ashkenazi Jew of anti-Semitic depictions with his drooping shoulders and his ears that stuck out.

He did a bit of this and a bit of that, what the *Encyclopaedia Britannica* calls odd jobs. His main means of income was provided by the market on Sixpions-Borguèze Square. In spite of his weak constitution, he helped merchants unload their trucks and set up their stands; then at the end of the market day, he helped them do all this again in the opposite direction.

One market day, people from the Jewish community (who were already helping out his large and poor family) tell him that the synagogue of the small town of Troisillons-Audouze is looking for a *schames,* a lay clerk.

Rosenberg feels his destiny taking a turn for the better. He obviously doesn't make the mistake of going directly to apply at Troisillons-Audouze. He goes to see all the Jews he is acquainted with, all credible persons with good reputations. He asks them for recommendations, introductions, not to mention information: who knows the people in charge of the synagogue at Troisillons-Audouze? It's only when he is properly equipped with promises, letters, and words that he goes to this small town near Troyes.

Rosenberg is preceded by a number of phone calls supporting him, and he is well received by the rabbi, the president of the community, and the treasurer. They are all quite friendly, and when Rosenberg wants to show them the letters of recommendation, they politely push them aside as they give him flattering and meaningful looks: we don't need them, we know you, we have heard about you, we are among friends . . . forget it.

The interview goes the same way, a friendly talk among equals. Visibly, they like Rosenberg. Finally, there's the written exam. Just a formality, not really necessary for someone like him . . .

And it's here that catastrophe hits. Rosenberg is quasi-illiterate. I say "quasi" rather than entirely, because no Jew (the people of the book—you know the tune they sing to us from our earliest childhood . . . Long live oral tradition!) can be truly illiterate . . . really. But he makes incredible mistakes when he writes, manhandling simple words, sprinkling commas here and there without any rhyme or reason, putting periods in the middle of sentences, showing a total ignorance of grammar—and all this with a horrible slowness and while sticking his tongue out sideways and biting it like a schoolchild. When it comes time to sign his name, what a nightmare! It takes him three tries, as he laboriously rounds up his loops, embellishes his downstrokes, caresses his upstrokes.

The leaders of the community can't believe their eyes. They ask Rosenberg to leave the room while they are deliberating.

"Even if he's only a *schames,* he has to know how to write."

"But why should he need writing to set out the chairs, open and close doors, distribute prayer books . . ."

"Exactly, and what is he going to distribute if he reads as badly as he writes? And how will he be able to take messages? No, the *schames* of a self-respecting community, and moreover one so close to Troyes, Rachi's town, can't be illiterate. We should help him. He's a very nice young man, and obviously he's far from being an idiot."

It was decided that Rosenberg was not to be hired, but he was to receive a sizable sum so that he could get a teacher at Troyes to give him spelling and grammar lessons.

Rosenberg was disappointed that he did not get the job, but he did not go look for a teacher. And it is at this point that we can mark the death of Rosenberg the *schnorrer-looser* and the beginning of his second life.

With the money he received he bought himself a cart and a permit, and the following Wednesday he could be seen in the market, his beloved market, proud, beaming, selling lettuce, beans, garlics (i.e., plural of garlic—like fishes and deers, subtleties of language known only in the newly minted English of immigrants awaiting their green cards),* scallions, and radishes. He had bought these vegetables from a widow of his acquaintance whom he knew to grow produce of exceptional quality but whose ailing legs did not let her stand in the market for hours. They were the finest vegetables in the area, the freshest, most appetizing ones. Rosenberg knew it, and his choice was well thought out.

All his produce was sold well before the market closing time. Rosenberg was no longer a *looser*. And even less a *schnorrer*. The next day, he bought twice as much produce . . . Soon he came to be known in all the market; he had acquired a reputation. Very quickly he was able to buy a small, beat-up pickup truck to carry produce from the widow's field to the market; soon he hired a helper to help the old woman, who couldn't grow enough; soon he bought the widow's land; soon he bought the adjacent field; soon he was selling to the two biggest wholesale food markets of the town; soon he became the partner of an industrial grower of industrial chickens; soon he left France to settle permanently in America; soon, after twenty years, he was the king of agri-food, a multimillionaire, and more.

One day Rosenberg had to go from Tucson, Arizona, where he lived, to Berlin. He was accompanied by his wife, a superb fake-platinum blonde from a several-generations Texas family who had moved to Arizona. (To go to Germany posed no problem to Moïse

---

*This statement reflects the author's own experience as an immigrant to France, and I have Americanized it by using "awaiting their green cards" instead of the literal translation "paperless waiting to be regularized." In the original French text there's a flurry of hilarious plurals formed by following rules rather than their many exceptions in usage (and, as with *aulx* in French and its equivalent—"garlics"—in English, the rules are sometimes correct even though rarely spoken). To speak a language according to the rules rather than the many exceptions to those rules indicates that the language was consciously learned rather than acquired in childhood (Biro personal communication). — *Trans.*

Rosenberg. It was only money and money has no odor, and even if it did, it would be a nice fresh smell. It was money that had been recycled, denazified; it was postwar marks, brand-new, very pretty, very expensive. He was just careful not to shake anyone's hand. Let's not get fixated on these petty acts of cowardice, these enormous stupidities, these ridiculous contradictions, these miniscule acts of hypocrisy, these stupid deals . . . Haven't you too . . . and we . . . well . . .) Rosenberg was supposed to sign, in the ex-new capital of this strange country, a **very big** contract with a **very big** corporation (a **global** one of course) dealing in leather. All of the negotiations had already been done by his staff—the only thing still needed was the boss's **solemn signature.** The twenty-six-page contract, read and reread by an army of lawyers from both sides is on the table. Rosenberg is supposed to sign the last page of each of the three copies. He is handed a gold Mont Blanc fountain pen; he takes it and begins laboriously to sign, to draw, to correct, to calligraphy, to cross out, to embellish, equalize, underline Mmmmmoïïïïssse Rooooosenbbbergggg, pulls out his tongue, bites on it—this whole process takes a short twenty-five minutes for the two words, an eternity with a watch in hand. Everyone is horribly uncomfortable, a frightful silence permeates the room. Then it's done. But he still has to put his initials on the bottom of each page and sign the other two copies. It's a nightmare; no one present will ever forget it, ever—except for the emperor of the agri-food business, the king of wheat and corn (genetic and transgenetic), the duke of dairy products and leather, the prince of nonalcoholic drinks, and the owner of half the castles in the Bordeaux region. He doesn't have to worry: he has a writer for English and another one for French in addition to his two trilingual secretaries . . .

"Herr Rosenberg, what an incredible success you've had," the slightly drunk president of the global corporation was to tell him later, at the end of dinner. "Can you just imagine where you would be today if you knew how to read and write properly?"

"Certainly, Mr. Schmitt. I would be the *schames* of the Troisillons-Audouze synagogue, near Troyes."

[I I]

In the course of his trip to Europe, Rosenberg went to see his family near Troyes. He had not returned for the last twenty years— a very long time. He had brought his parents over for two visits to America, then for vacations, but he had not seen his brothers and sisters. It was a good opportunity to get the whole family together, at least those who were still alive. He thus rented a car (an American one, he only knew how to drive big, automatic American cars) and, with his wife in the suicide seat, he returned to the place of his birth.

Nothing had changed. The old apartment building was still standing and still located as it had been, somewhere between poverty and misery. This because, as the friendly reader might have guessed, the Rosenbergs were poor Jews. They had many children, and the father, now dead, had been all his working life a petty book-keeper in a cooperative winery and had not earned enough to maintain the building. Moïse had sweetened this miserable dwelling with dollars sent from America. Though Moïse didn't know how to write, he did have a sense of family duty—like all of us, needless to say. The small wooden bench was still in front of the building, under the awning, on the left of the entry door, and on the bench, as if he hadn't moved one inch for the last twenty years, sat Moïse's kid brother, Simon, smoking. When Moïse Rosenberg had bid farewell to his family before leaving for the United States, he had left Simon seated on the same bench on the street, in the same way as now, his legs stretched out in front of him, leaning against the wall, his Gauloise in his mouth. But when the white Cadillac came to a stop and his brother and his wife got out, Simon jumped up, filled with admiration.

"Moïse, but . . ." He was speechless. He had never been seen so agitated. He barely let his brother greet the others, go up, and tour the apartment.

"So tell me, how did you do it?"

Simon, two years younger than Moïse, had never done anything in his life.

While Moïse, the *schnorrer,* was striving to amass some pennies
at the market,
Simon wasn't trying anything.
Seated on the bench,
protected from the wind,
from the rain,
from the snow,
from all stress,
from all feelings,
from all resentment,
from anything apt to trouble one's mind, thus to shorten a human life,
very calm, very happy, he went with the flow. His parents, and
the community, took care of him as best they could—rather
badly, that is, but he was contented with very little.
Simon wanted for nothing.
The street, the spectacle of the street, the people, the ever-
changing sky . . . Dressed the same way in summer and winter,
with a cap, a gray jacket, corduroy pants, a checked shirt, and a
necktie . . . Actually not quite, for in winter he added a big
woolen scarf around his neck. From time to time his brothers and
sisters, his parents, told him to go to work. People at city hall and
also from the Jewish community even mentioned possible jobs to
him—but Simon's nonchalance, inertia, and indolence soon dis-
couraged even the most well-meaning would-be helpers. Simon
never said no; he never refused any suggestions, he even ex-
pressed gratefulness. Simply, he never made the slightest effort to
obtain the smallest of jobs. He simply never called up the person
who was awaiting his phone call; simply, he never kept any of the
appointments the well-meaning people made for him. In this
way, he was able to keep the only spot he liked, the bench in front
of the house, and pursue the only activity that interested him, to
sit on that bench and smoke his cigarette while watching people
go by.
But now, the arrival of his brother, the only human being besides

his parents for whom he felt some affection and even interest, totally agitated him.

"Moïse," he says to his brother whom he had not seen in twenty years, "how did you do it? This dream car . . . I've never seen any like this . . . and this chick, I mean this woman, I mean this lady, is she your wife?"

The chick in question didn't understand one word of French. Her long platinum hair reached to her butt. As for her butt itself and the rest of her, they were as comely as could be. I won't give a detailed description. I'm sure my readers can imagine them for themselves. The poor blonde thought that an American woman in Europe was expected to resemble Jayne Mansfield, and so she did. At any rate her image was totally ungraspable, incomprehensible, it was in no way assimilable to a European Jew whose vision of the world was constructed out of the sole spectacle of a nine-hundred-foot-long segment of a street in the outskirts of an urban area of Champagne.

Simon continues with his questions:

"But how were you able to make so much money in so little time?"

The car and the woman—and what a car and what a woman!—signified wealth not only to Simon but to the whole street. As to time—what could twenty years mean to someone who understands space only through a street and time only through unchanging duration?

Moïse is touched by so much naïveté. It might not be too late for Simon to change his ways; after all he is his brother . . .

"My fortune is much larger than this. The car, that's nothing. Besides it's not even mine. I have two others in Arizona. As for the woman . . . it's true she requires lots of money. But I can afford it. You see, Simon, before anything else, I have to tell you that it was very hard to earn all this. I began life as a *looser*, and I was stuck on the market square of Sixpions-Borguèze like a *schnorrer*. I've had to work my buns off to get out of that situation. I had to do a lot of thinking, to be ruthless at times. I had to crush the meanies that you sometimes find blocking your way, and I had to work and work, from morning till night and from night till morning, all the time. So this is how it happened: with the money the community gave me I bought myself a cart and a spot in the market."

"I remember," says Simon.

"All right, I'm only explaining to you how I did it. Shall I continue?"

"Yes!" exclaims Simon, full of enthusiasm.

"Then I bought the best produce of the area from the Montaignier widow—do you remember her? She couldn't go sell it, because of her ailing legs. And since she liked me, she told me all her growing secrets, the tricks she used, all her techniques. I remembered it all—it wasn't easy, it was new for me."

"Yes, and then?"

"I sold this superb produce at a very low price. This drew many buyers. What I lost on individual items, I made up on the whole, and then some. And I came to have steady customers by maintaining the quality."

Simon didn't understand everything, but no matter. He was hanging on the words of his beloved older brother.

"And then?"

"Then I moved; you must remember, it caused a ruckus at home, and then, when I made quite a bit of money, instead of spending it I bought Mrs. Montaignier's land, as she wasn't able to cultivate it any longer. I hired two workers for the vegetables and the fruit trees, I bought a pickup truck to carry my merchandise to the market, where I rented a bigger place, and I took a second salesman along. Like that, between the two of us and the truck, we were able to work every day, going from market to market, and not only twice a week to the one on Sixpions-Borguèze Square. But we worked like dogs. At dawn, we picked up the merchandise, we cleaned it to make it presentable, we loaded up the truck, set up the booth at the market, we sold, we yelled, we took in the money, we haggled, then we cleared the booth, put things away, cleaned up, dismantled our booth, stored the stuff, fixed the old truck . . ."

"Amazing, Moïse, amazing!" Simon is getting even more excited.

"Then I bought the parcel next to mine, then another, but instead of hiring another worker, I offered a commission to the two that I already had."

"And did they agree?"

"But of course! They were delighted. They had confidence in me, they banked on me."

"And then?"

Simon sits down, forcing his brother to sit down with him, and he listens with his mouth wide open.

"Then, I began to sell to all the supermarkets of the area under the label Veggiegold. For the same price, customers could have produce and eggs that were very fresh, very beautiful. I had low prices! So they bought only my stuff. But I can't begin to tell you how much work, how many bribes it took to convince the supermarkets."

"That's incredible; go on . . ."

"I became partners with a fruit juice maker who bought the unsold remainders of my produce. Then he bought Veggiegold from me for lots of money and begged me to stay with the firm, as he realized that without me, the golden produce would turn to ugly mud. But I had gotten all my knowledge from old Mrs. Montaignier."

"Go on!" begs an overexcited Simon.

"The fruit juice maker had lands and vineyards scattered all over the area. I then forced him to raise my commission, and I oversaw all of his agricultural enterprises. And then, as I had some spare time, I became partners with a raiser of industrial chickens . . ."

"What's an industrial chicken?" asked Simon.

"It's a chicken that never sees the light of day, that can't move, that is born, eats, and gets killed to be eaten. It's, if you will, like an object, a balloon that is being pumped up. And it costs next to nothing. An egg hatches in the electrical incubator without the need for any hen, then it's fed very cheap chemically processed feed, and you sell these chickens frozen, to international outfits, everywhere in the world. Well, it's true, your profit margin is one hell of a small one, but you still make a buck."

"Moïse, what's a profit margin?"

Moïse explains it to him.

"I must be dreaming—and then?"

"Then I became associated with other agri-food businesses. Veal, that's good: you can sell its meat for more than that of a cow and it costs you less than the cow because you don't need to raise it; then you sell its skin to make leather, and its hooves to make fertilizer or luxury beauty products. And by then you're already wealthy. But you slaved, and how! You're exhausted but you're already in the U.S., of course. It's only there that one can really make money. You kill yourself on the job, all right, but you can *make it*. You need to travel all the time, you keep on getting up at dawn to catch your plane, your train, you drive a million miles. America is very big— you have no idea—you're wiped out, stressed out . . . but! At the same time you're investing in all related areas: in corn, peanuts, feed; you invest in stocks left and right, in Nestlé . . ."

"And then?"

"Then you work in a different way, you watch over your stocks, you call your broker five times a day, you send faxes, e-mails, you surf the 'net all day long so as not to miss a good deal, you control your employees, you . . ."

Simon wasn't understanding a thing.

"Yes, I understand, but then?"

"That's when, you see, Simon, you can become really wealthy. You have several cars, a superb house with a swimming pool, you have already married a blonde like mine, you have almost all that . . ."

"And then, Moïse? Go on!"

Simon is getting breathless.

"Hey, calm down a little! You're getting on my nerves with all your 'thens'! Well then you're the king of the agri-food business or of whatever, *when you've made it, man;* at that point you're totally burnt out. You've worked all your life like no dog would. Then you're a success story. You get what everybody is always looking for: rest, peace. Well yes, you can finally sit on a bench in front of your house, light up a smoke, stretch out your legs, just like that, do nothing, simply look at the street and take a deep breath, happy."

TWO FRIENDS

BERNARD AND JEAN-MARIE had been partners for a long time. The first was very good at business and public relations while the other had the gift for abstraction and was very skillful with his hands. They opened a business that installed and repaired electrical devices. Bernard sought out customers, solicited from companies, scouted out building sites, took care of promotion and advertising, oversaw the bookkeeping, contacted banks, did the payroll. As for Jean-Marie, he researched new technologies, bought the required materials, hired workers, drew up bids, and supervised the various jobs and building sites. Their business was going well because, in addition to their undeniable competence, which some people labeled exceptional, they were hard workers, they were honest in their dealings with each other, and they stood by each other in difficult as well as in good times.

After a certain number of years, Jean-Marie became interested in computers. Since he did well at everything he got involved in, he turned into an ace of the Mac and a master of the PC. The two partners thus changed their business, which they turned into a very sought-out and appreciated office computers repair service—their increasingly numerous repairpersons, equipped with cell phones, were crisscrossing Paris on their scooters ready to respond to the call of panicky customers, victims of monitor wipeout. Bernard and Jean-Marie were making a very good and honest living. Bernard was attuned to subtleties, was gifted in knowing how to approach and talk to people. And yet, the more he had to do with people, the more he despised them, they and their nest, society. As to Jean-Marie, he was an unflinching optimist; he loved life and nothing could take away his faith in a bright technological future where human beings would be freed from all menial tasks.

One day, Bernard's wife realized that the partnership of Bernard and Jean-Marie had lasted twenty-five years. She mentioned it to her husband, who right away decided to celebrate the event with a dinner for four. So they did. A table was reserved in a very good restaurant for the two partners and their spouses.

The meal was worthy of the reputation of the house. We won't describe the menu; we are in France after all and won't insult our readers, their imaginations, their culture, their knowledge. We know that all they have to do is close their eyes to immediately see on their mental table all the appetizers, the entrees, the desserts, the wines they are particularly fond of, the rarest, most succulent, and most expensive ones.

Bernard and Jean-Marie were not big drinkers, but they rose to the occasion. This time, for this anniversary meal, they overdid it. The wines were called (we might as well own up to it after all) Château Lafite and Petrus—and the cigar at the end of the meal ("One time does not a habit make," and the ladies were indulgent) was a Château Haut-Brion from Davidoff . . . They started out telling old stories from the time when they began without money (they had met each other in the army at age twenty). As the evening wore on they told all the stories about bad customers, bad payers, bad taxes, the people they had met, funny suppliers, nutty employees. Their wives were bored out of their gourds. They knew all the stories by heart, even that of the check in the name of Monsieur Einstein, and that of the check engraved on a wooden plank and beautifully gift-wrapped, and the case of the musically inclined office messenger and the bookkeeper who was always too hot.

"Particularly you know where," interjected Jean-Marie, and the two friends almost choked from laughter.

The time had come to go home, to begin the next twenty-five years. As he was about to get up, an unsteady Bernard grabbed hold of Jean-Marie's lapel and, as he became totally serious, looked him straight in the eye and told him:

"Jean-Marie, I have to confess something. It has weighed on me for a long time, but I never dared. I should have; we are really such good friends; the sky, hiccup hiccup, the sky of our friendship has never, never, ever, been darkened by any cloud. Listen, you're my partner, I have to tell you: I'm Jewish."

There's a heavy silence. Everyone looks embarrassed. Jean-Marie frees the lapel of his jacket from Bernard's hand and says very calmly:

"Me too, I have to confess something to you: I have a limp."

HISTORY

MOSHE WAS DYING. He was very old. Very, very old—no one knew exactly what his real age was. One hundred years? More? His official papers, his many passports, his countless ID cards in countless languages, his French social security sheet, his life insurance, his bank account, and many other documents, papers, certificates, which he was able and had to (mostly had to) have drawn, established, filled, bought, falsified, stolen, recopied, found, and got hold of in the course of his very long life, showed an imaginary date of birth that a Polish police officer with an overly humorous sense of humor had inscribed on a useless paper. At the time of his birth, the birth of a Jewish child was not entered in the registers of the community—but where was that community, where were its registers? And the country, did it still exist? And even the sky, the clouds, the air, the smells of the towns, the towns themselves, and the fields, did they still exist? Life, LIFE, to put it simply, was not the same: neither better nor worse, just different.

Moshe loved it. Life, that is. In spite of . . . in spite of Polish officers, multiple and contradictory ID papers, useless documents whether they be free or exorbitant, real or fake, compromising or indispensable, suspect or necessary. He loved life in spite of his infi-

nite despair about human beings and their condition. He particularly loved the city, the Parisian asphalt, the diversity of the faces he
encountered; he loved bad weather and sunshine too, the heat and
the cold, looking at the sky, feeling the rain, reading his paper in
Yiddish in an old armchair (not necessarily *his* old armchair, but an
old armchair), going to the café to play cards with his friends
(whose numbers were dwindling), eating and drinking simple
things with strong tastes, making business deals as if it were a game,
feeling generous when giving a bit of money to his grandchildren
or to charity. When he was young, he had loved beautiful women
. . . Life, that was pretty much what it was all about. As to God?
Very little . . .

And now he was on his deathbed. He had no illness, he was simply dying of old age; his cells, his mucous membranes, his bones,
his nerves, his blood vessels, his muscles knew each other too well,
so much they had rubbed on each other, and now they were too
tired to work together. They had nothing left to learn, though even
God had been studying on the seventh day.

Golda, his wife, was seated on the edge of the bed, and was desperately trying to think. She was trying to imagine what life was going to be, might be and become, without Moshe. She was Moshe's
age, or about. Who knew? They had lived more than seventy years
together—how could she think of life differently? Without Moshe?
She realized she couldn't, that she wasn't able even to think of
herself alone, to conjure up an image in which she would be seated
in the living room, alone, or in the evening, watching TV or cooking
some food just for herself, or standing in the kitchen and chopping
onions *just for herself.*

Golda was giving her husband the damp washcloth, the glass of
water, the useless medication; she changed the radio channel when
Moshe asked her, turning the dial from Radio Shalom to Libertar-
ian Radio ("nuts," "dreamers"—but Moshe felt affection for them
and their totally amateurish station) and then to France Musique,
then classical music radio, and finally "Kurt-Nazi" Radio (in real
life misnamed "Radio Courtoisie") so as to get excited and call

them *fachos* (actually this newfangled French term wasn't in his vocabulary; he said "fascists") and finally back to Radio Shalom to begin the whole circuit again. She read him articles that interested him, fluffed up his pillows, aired the room—there wasn't much to do.

But wait.

Wait for what?

The children will visit tomorrow.

Moshe spoke little, but he did speak.

"Tell me, Golda, do you remember the horrible pogrom in our village in 1905, when the Cossacks raped my sister and set the stable on fire, and we had to hide in the baker's attic?"

"Of course, I remember it. But why are you tormenting yourself with this? It happened so long ago . . . we are no longer in Ukraine, we are in France. There are no more Cossacks. We live in peace."

"Tell me, Golda, were you with me then?"

Tears come to Golda's eyes.

"Of course, I was with you."

There is a long, very long silence. Moshe has dozed off. Then suddenly, as if he were coming out of a dream:

"And tell me, Golda, do you remember when the Bolsheviks were looking for young men to conscript to fight against the Whites, in 1918, and found me and beat me half to death?"

Golda remembers it all. She remembers that Moshe was gone for a long time and she remembers the state he was in when he came back from the war.

Moshe has turned silent again. And then:

"Were you with me then?"

Golda has always been at Moshe's side, then as well.

"And the Poles, do you remember? When they were looking for Jews who had been on the Reds' side? When they locked us up in the synagogue and beat us all up? Tell me, Golda, were you there too?"

Golda is exhausted. She doesn't want to remember all these horrors. Particularly not now. And besides . . .

"Yes, I was there. I was always with you, Moshe."

"And in forty-two, in the Lemberg ghetto? Do you remember the filth, the vermin, the dead bodies, the way we were tortured to tell where our money was hidden. Ha! what a joke, our money! Our . . ."

Moshe chokes on a fit of coughing. Golda lifts his head and makes him drink.

". . . our terror to remain there . . . our ignorance of the horrendous future . . . Were you with me in the Lemberg ghetto?"

"Of course I was with you. But try to sleep a little, please. Stop thinking of all this. Think instead of all the good things; we've had so much happiness . . ."

But the old man stops her. He is impatient, as if driven by an urgent need to remember, to relive everything . . .

"After that, at Maidanek, in the camp, do you remember the horror? The forced labor, death all around us, the absence of hope? It's a miracle we came out of it alive, isn't it? And in what a state! Oh God, the life we've had to lead."

Oh no, not Maidanek. But Golda knew they were getting to it, she knew her husband couldn't help talk about it.

"There too, were you with me at Maidanek?"

"At Maidanek, like everywhere else, I was with you. I was in the women's camp."

Moshe falls asleep. That was too much. Golda is frightened. But he's breathing; he's a bit agitated, but he's breathing—and then he opens his big eyes, turns his head toward Golda, looks at her a long time before asking her:

"Tell me in the fifties, when the Communists again took everything from us and deported us to the countryside with the children, five to a room, in the middle of cornfields, were you there?"

Why is he asking this question? Can't he remember?

"Yes, I was there," says Golda.

Moshe continues, breathlessly, as if in a hurry:

"And then in Paris, when we finally thought we had found peace and security, in rue des Rosiers,* the shooting at Goldenberg's, do

---

*A Jewish neighborhood in Paris. — *Trans.*

you remember it as clearly as I do? When we had to throw ourselves down on the ground and await a stray bullet, await our last hour? Were you with me at the Goldenberg restaurant, rue des Rosiers, in Paris?"

"Yes, my love, my Moshe, I was there, at your table, at Goldenberg's; there too I was with you. I've always been with you, always."

Beads of sweat begin to form on Moshe's forehead. He is quiet and contemplates the ceiling. There's a deep silence, as if all of a sudden Moshe has found peace, calm, and serenity. He gives a long look to Golda and finally tells her in a low, matter-of-fact voice:

"You see, Golda, I think you were bad luck."

THE TOURIST

[I]

TAÏEB IS DEAD.* Everybody must die, but Taïeb was too young, in the flower of youth. He had no disease, no vice, not a single bad habit—that's perhaps what he died of.

There's so much that can be said about someone, so many ways of explaining a person, and people certainly don't deprive themselves of it. But they merely clothe other people with their own problems. Taïeb came from a large family and had lots of friends, but no one really knew him, because it's not possible to really know somebody. We already know so little about our own selves . . .

Taïeb is dead . . . in fact there's not much to talk about, which did not prevent his friends and his enemies from talking and talking about it.

Taïeb is dead. People could think whatever they wanted, but he had pleased God and he went directly to Heaven. He sang the glory of the Lord, seated on his right, hallelujah from morning till night—except there's neither morning nor night in this kingdom of pure

*This is a tale told by French Sephardic Jews of North African origins.

souls. Thus it was hallelujah all the time—even though obviously there was no time.

And boredom, did it exist? Since there was no time, no evening, no morning? Well yes, there was boredom. How was that possible? We don't know. It's one of the divine mysteries. And Taïeb became seriously bored on the right of the Lord. Praises, to sing praises (not from morning to night, not all the time, we have already explained this), to sing, simply, to sing—after an eternity of this, Taïeb became fed up. From "time to time" as we say on earth, during pauses, our Taïeb would discreetly lift up the heavy curtain behind his seat, a curtain made of dreams, clouds, blessings, brocade, cashmere, beatitude, prayer, and red velvet; it was made up of cloth woven, embroidered, smoothed out by the angels.

And what did he see?

He saw Hell, all the way down, far, far, and yet very near (there's no space either in Paradise). Music reached his ears, a music that was sweet and infinitely beautiful, a mixture of Patrick Bruel, Joe Dassin, Enrico Macias, Dalida, Mozart, and Andrea Bocelli.* Charming young women, scantily clad, were dancing lasciviously (if there's no time and no space, how can movement exist? Do not ask us to explain those mysteries . . .). Taïeb could contemplate at leisure how the men among the damned were lying down on silk cushions and were voluptuously caressing the magnificent naked forms of the infernal barmaids while these poured them drinks in glasses of fluorescent colors.

Other damned souls were playing backgammon, bridge, and other games Taïeb had been fond of in his lifetime. Some, in a corner, busied themselves around splendid, brightly painted racing cars. They were repairing them, shining them, and were trying

---

*These are all stars popular with the French Sephardic Jews who had to emigrate in great number from North Africa to France (Biro personal communication). The description of musical instruments and the names of the drinks that follow, however, are the fruit of the author's imagination and at times of the translator's imaginative translation.—*Trans.*

them out. There were Facel-Vegas, MGs, Porsches, Mercedes 300 SLs. (Taïeb, who had owned a little Peugeot 104 on earth, had a weakness for fast luxury cars.)

Some others yet again were organizing soccer games in which both teams would win at the same time.

Some of the denizens of Hell were lounging at the side of a pool while sipping turquoise-colored cocktails with phosphorescent purple straws; some were diving from a very high diving board, but their dives were very slow, soft as feathers flying in the evening breeze at La Goulette. Others yet practiced playing tennis, and they hit each ball powerfully across the net, barely skimming it, and these balls were easily returned in the same manner by their opponents.

We could go on, but Taïeb had let the curtain drop. "Hallelujah," he sings as he rejoins the celestial choir, "Hosanna!" "Baruch Ata, Elohenu!" and also "Hail Mary, Full of Grace" (there is no good or bad religion in heaven), and were these sung in Burmese? in Japanese? in Finnish? in Kurdish? Wrong! There are no differences in Paradise: there's only one single language; it unites everyone. And then, from time to time, a quick look down below, toward the poor damned . . . Sounds of music, of the gwortz, of the istulki, of the gompelnno (oh, the sweet rubbing sounds of the gompelnno!), and the drinks, the ozaltaks (Taïeb could clearly see their crimson color darkened with black pepper), the velvet hammers, the Juliette on the lips, the shaggy catajios, and there was surfing on parallel waves breaking down evenly on the beach . . .

And again, looking back toward the Lord.

Taïeb was in hell, figuratively speaking.

After a length of time (again! How can we invoke duration on earth without talking of time; how can we feel the unfolding of events without having recourse to the notion of duration? No matter—you and I are damned for the time being to be on earth), thus after a length of time, Taïeb couldn't stand it anymore. He was looking down more and more often . . . His hands would join in prayer, hallelujah . . . Then he would steal a guilty look down toward the guilty . . . On one of the days off, Taïeb requested a special meeting with the Creator.

He was not available. He could not be disturbed. He was busy as usual every seventh day performing various corrections in the divine order of the world. What can I tell you? Do we know this? Can we understand it? Was it to coordinate the travels of the ladybugs of the village of Siófok-Tisztviselötelep by Lake Balaton in Hungary with those of solar system number 153? Let us imagine that this was it, so we can be reassured. The world is governed. Someone is taking care of it. It doesn't seem that way, from our earthly perspective, but . . .

So, instead of talking personally with the Lord, Taïeb got an interview with the archangel holding a post somewhat similar to a secretary of state. This archangel warned him:

"Be careful: it might not appear so, but Hell is really Hell!"

Taïeb insisted. Just once, just to see for himself; just one day in Hell, and then, hallelujah, better than ever, hallelujah . . .

He was granted permission to go for the duration of one Sabbath.

Orders having been given from on high downward (Paradise is extremely hierarchized), a helicopter was put at Taïeb's disposal and he landed softly on Hell's heliport. He was welcomed by young hostesses (all blondes without exception) in vaporous uniforms who led him to the changing room, where he took off his all-white celestial attire (a cross between a toga and a tallith) for a lighter outfit, one more informal, more infernal.

It was a day even more beautiful than Taïeb could have imagined. Men of his age who resembled his school friends, but in adult forms, were discussing politics on the café patios, and they spontaneously invited Taïeb to participate in the discussion. The young women were sweeter, more obliging, more submissive than when he was looking at them from above, and one of them reminded him of his elementary school teacher, whom he had been in love with. To the racing cars there were now added motorcycles, motorboats; to the tennis matches was added fishing, in which talking and very polite fish happily offered themselves to fishermen; there were outdoor barbecues, and finally an evening of TV-watching with a film by Louis de Funès! The food dishes served had new tastes that still reminded him of his mother's cooking and, in the swimming pool, it was possible to stay indefinitely submerged, as one could breathe underwater.

Then one of the hostesses gently took Taïeb by the arm and led him to the waiting helicopter.

And he was already, again, at his eternally designated place, on the right of the Lord, in front of the curtain, singing, praying, ceremonializing, blending, psalmodizing, saluting, thanking, incensing, prostrating, kneeling, wallowing, praising, hallelujahing to his heart's content. It did have its charms, but . . .

And our poor Taïeb would lift the heavy curtain more and more often, to contemplate the infernal spectacle whose reality he now knew. Friends, women, body, flesh, the absence of any duty, of any need, food, drinks, sun, the sea, rest, carefreeness, relaxation . . . This was everything that he had sought on earth in vain, always . . .

You guessed it: he wasn't able to resist. He asked again to see the Lord and of course his request was denied, and he was seen by the same archangel as previously. But this time, Taïeb asked for permission to permanently go to Hell.

"Have you really thought this through? Forever, in Hell, means forever, for all of eternity. There is no possibility of returning here, no matter what. You can cry, beg, scream—you will have to stay."

Taïeb didn't care. He knew what he knew. He wasn't going to beg to come back.

"Do you know that since Paradise was established, that is, since the beginning of eternity, only a few million of the dead, thus practically no one, have asked to leave it for Hell? Think about it! There must be good reasons."

But Taïeb was determined. He didn't even need to weigh the pros and cons.

"I'm really decided."

"All right! You asked for it!" exclaimed the archangel.

A trap door opened like a toothless mouth, and Taïeb fell head-first. No soft helicopter landing this time . . . He crashed on the ground. He tried to get up, as if he had fallen from a tree, but, to his horror, he noticed he had broken his arm in the fall.

"I need a doctor!" he bellowed.

"Here's one!"

A sort of little devil, a minuscule homunculus, or rather a femi-nicula about thirty inches high, black, with goat horns, hairy, with heavy dangling breasts and two translucid winglets, was looking at him, sneering. She was holding a pitchfork-needle-sting in her hand, which she plunged with a great guffaw of laughter into Taïeb's broken arm, at the precise spot of the break. He screamed. His scream drew a hundred more of the little female monsters through a wall of fire as high as several buildings; they threw him to the ground and had him tied up in a split second; then one after an-other, they began to tear pieces of his skin, of his flesh, with their teeth and various instruments, pincers, pliers, scissors. Where were the submissive hostesses? Taïeb's pain was horrendous, and the she-devils wouldn't let go—on the contrary. It lasted . . . an eter-nity, of course. Taïeb's cries were met with the sneering of the femi-niculae. Then with a terrifying metal noise there burst out of the wall of flames an enormous black locomotive. The she-devils opened its red-hot boiler and ordered Taïeb:

"Get in!"

Taïeb, crushed, terrified, was still able to articulate an inarticu-late inhuman scream:

"I want to talk to the boss!"

With these words the wall of flames opened up to allow the entrance—Frightening, Terrifying, Indescribable, and quasi-Incommensurable—

of the Devil himself.

He flipped over the pitiful Taïeb with the tip of his toe, looked at him with contempt, and then told him in an unknown language that Taïeb immediately understood:

"Tourism and immigration are not the same thing!"

[I I]

There is another version of the drama I just told you. It's not a communist version but rather a Stalinist one (the two are not the same! We should not confuse a generous idea with horror . . .).

In this version, which has to be told with an Eastern European accent, the French Sephardi Taïeb is called Fischer, the music that rises up to him from Hell is that of Bartók, of Leonard Cohen, of Kurt Weill, of Schubert, of Stockhausen; it's czardas, waltzes, mazurkas; the damned play the violin and chess. When Fischer, seated like a good boy to the right of the Lord, looks longingly downward, to Hell, what does he see? Peasants and intellectuals, bankers, landlords, steelworkers having a friendly discussion while seated around a table and giving each other nonstop praises. And when Fischer gets permission to go down to Hell for a day, he discovers a fraternal society which is no longer a society but a fraternity where the happy damned from the countryside and the towns are paid according to their needs, not in money but in the goods required for happiness; where none of the damned is exploited by others; where women are equal to men; where there are no longer races, skin colors, nationalities, minorities and majorities; where justice doesn't even need to triumph because it is as evident as air and water; where all the means of production are held in common; where production doesn't even exist any longer, as obedient machines replace the backbreaking work of the damned . . . Fischer wants, wants, how should we put it? desires, aspires, requires . . . he WANTS to live in this happy Hell that reminds him of the image of the Paradise he had imagined . . . But watch out, sensitive readers, the fall will be terrible.

Listen:

On earth our poor Fischer had been used to all kinds of changes, every deception, all the physical and psychological torments that this bloodied century had reserved, on the one hand, for Jews,*

*At this point of the story, a listener interrupted me by yelling: "and what about all the rest?"

and, on the other, for the inhabitants of Eastern Europe, and thus, particularly for Eastern European Jews. But what happens to him goes well beyond his extensive experience: he has barely landed in Hell for an eternal stay when he's terrorized, interrogated, tortured by little devils who call him dirty Jew, idiot Polack, rotten bourgeois, social-traitor vermin, garbage of an exploiter, capitalist jerk, filthy kulak, peasant mud, starver of the people, Bolshevik, and other kind words he was only too familiar with. When he asks where are the happy peasants, the elated workers, he is answered with the most horrendous tortures even as he is forced to confess, sign, denounce, deny, forsake, silence, shut up, scream, repeat, testify, accuse, own up, forget, psalmodize, applaud, hoot, point out, dissimulate, remember . . . Fischer knows that he has nothing to lose, since in this absolute that is Hell, there are no more emergency exits than there are diminutives, comparatives, or superlatives. So he gathers up his courage and screams out his demand to see the boss. And when the Devil appears in person, our poor hero addresses the Great Torturer in these terms:

"But what is this? This isn't what you promised me! It's not what I learned, what I saw, heard, hoped for! I was misled, shamelessly misled!"

The great Red Devil emits an inarticulate yell that could be taken for either a guffaw of laughter or a threat and bends all the way down to the tiny, fooled militant, the rank-and-file Fischer, before belching out a single word:

"Prrrropaganda!"

TROUSERS

THE EDIFYING LITTLE STORY you are about to hear happens in a Paris neighborhood called Le Sentier [the path], locus of the Jewish clothing business. The two (Paris and Le Sentier) were blessed by the gods and particularly by the One in charge of blessing the Jews before other people. Before all others, without distinction of race, color, or creed, because he's a just and equitable God.

One morning a certain Shmuel gets an urgent phone call from his friend Moïse.

"Listen, Shmuel. Have I got a mega-top deal for you! You're my buddy; you're the first I'm offering it to. But you need to decide right away, otherwise I'll call Simon, because a deal like this one doesn't come twice a year, and I want my friend, rather than strangers, to take advantage of it."

"I understand," says Moïse. They know each other. They are both able to decipher a coded language, particularly when it's their native tongue. The preamble made it clear. Shmuel wants to quickly unload some sort of merchandise for a low price. What could it be?

"Listen, I have a lot of trousers for ten francs each. The brand is

Ochsenstier. You know, that German brand that lasts forever. Can you imagine? Ten francs. You can't find anything like that. It's for you, only for you."

Moïse is in a hurry, and he is fond of Shmuel. He doesn't want to waste time haggling over the price.

"All right, I'll buy them from you for five francs. I realize that I am doing you a favor. I'm buying them because it's you and you have problems. Someday you'll do the same for me."

"What are you talking about? What problem? Are you nuts? If you don't want them, you only need to say one word and I'll call . . ."

"Oh, stop it already. I told you it's okay at five francs. So it's okay. Just send them to me, that's all. Anything else? How are you doing otherwise?"

They keep on negotiating for a short while, perfunctorily; the negotiation is part of the trousers; it is sewn into them. Then the deal is concluded. Shmuel calls Simon almost before he is through hanging up after talking to Moïse.

"Say, Simon, do you want a fabulous deal? Like you never had before? You do know how much Ochsenschwein pants are sold for nowadays. Don't interrupt me please. I'm speaking as a friend. So tell me, do you know for how much? You don't know? Then there's no point in even talking to you. You won't get it. You won't even understand what I'll tell you, the gift I want to give you."

"Why do you want to give me a gift?" asks the other, surprised.

Shmuel answers:

"Because you're my brother. That's all. Do you mind? I still have a right to exist, no? I still have the right to give gifts? Or do I need special permits and seals and to pay a special gift tax? Okay, let me tell you: I have a lot of pants that I can sell you, just for you, for forty a pair. I repeat so that you'll understand, twenty francs for each, thus forty francs for each pair, yes. Do you want them or not? That's all—if not, it's no big deal . . ."

Simon is tired, but he still renegotiates the price, of course, you know the routine by heart. Tiredness or not. Otherwise no one would understand anything anymore; everyone would end up mistrusting everybody. Finally he says:

"All right, send them over."

And he right away calls Sidney, Momo's brother. Momo owes him money from way back when, that is, practically from forever.

"Hello, Hello, Sidney! It's Simon. How's it going? And your bro? I never see him lately. But that's not why I am calling you. I have a lot of pants for sale, a bargain, a rare deal, it just arrived from Germany, from Ochsenschwanzsuppe, can you just imagine the quality and cut. I'll give them to you for thirty francs a piece, rock bottom,* it's a done deal, don't think too long, otherwise . . ."

"What! You're threatening me? Me? I'll give you twenty-five francs."

Sidney never bargains. He is known for that. With him it's either yes or no.

"Okay, Sidney, don't thank me, please, don't thank me. And don't forget to say hello to your brother for me. And tell him to drop by one of these days. I'm quite fond of him, tell him."

Sidney might be a man of few words, but he does know how to count. He'll resell the whole package to Isaac, this blabbermouth who's always looking for good deals. He'll make his profit on the side, and he'll make his day with one phone call. And at the same time he'll have done a favor to Simon, to whom Momo, his idiot brother, has owed money since way back when, since no one can remember. Since always.

"Isaac? Hi, it's Sidney. You remember the other day you asked me to tell you about a deal, if I should hear of one. Well, this morning, I heard of a lot of trousers for forty francs apiece. And they are German O, you see, yes, a famous brand for a change. If you want, I'll save them for you before they get away."

Isaac wades into the sticky swamp of his explanations, tergiversations, negotiations, questions and answers, internal and external

---

*The French *moins cher tu meurs* means literally "any less ,you die"; it's a French Sephardic expression. — *Trans.*

interrogations, formidable soliloquies that Sidney doesn't listen to, and, knowing Isaac, simply puts the phone down on the desk and picks it up a few minutes later and says:

"So you're taking them or not?"

Isaac yet again drowns in his logorrhea.

"Listen, Isaac, answer me or I'm hanging up. Life is short. I'll give you five francs off. Answer me with one word: either 'yes,' and I'll send them to you today, or 'no,' and then I won't get angry, I'll just keep them for myself."

"You know Sidney that . . ."

"Hey, cut it out, Isaac, enough already. Is it yes or no?"

Isaac is in pain. What's going on? Certainly not a negotiation. How can one, like that, in two words . . . There's more to life than money. At the back of money, there are words, and at the back of the words, there're people, there's life, people's life . . . His father warned him, beware of silent people! He feels like refusing the deal. Is Sidney really a friend?

"All right, it's yes."

"Thanks, Isaac. It's sold. God bless.* Ciao, I'll take care of everything."

Isaac calls Max, an old buddy he seldom sees these days. In fact, Max avoids him, practically runs away from Isaac, who drives him crazy. When he recognizes his voice over the phone, he feels like hanging up but doesn't dare. That would be rude. But fearing the flood of Isaac's words, he interrupts him right away, and thus upsets him:

"Where are they and how much you want for them?"

"Listen, it's exceptional merchandise, from Ochsenwurm . . ."

"How much?"

Isaac likes to talk, but he isn't stupid. He is aware that he is getting on Max's nerves and this immediately, at the very beginning of

*The French *Cinq sur toi,* an Arabic and Sephardi expression literally meaning "five on you," is the spoken representation of a *hamsa,* a protective amulet depicting an open hand with the palm outward, signifying "good luck," "God bless you," etc. (Biro personal communication). — *Trans.*

the conversation. If he wants to make this deal, he has to put his cards on the table.

"Fifty francs, okay?"

"That's a lot, but I'll go for forty-five just because it's you."

"Oh, what a joke! That's a good one, too good! Stop it already! You're killing me!"—and he starts to talk again.

Max, by then a nervous wreck, hangs up without saying a word. Isaac calls him back, yells at him for his rudeness, and they conclude the deal for forty-seven francs and fifty centimes.

Max wonders what possessed him to get involved in this deal. He has never in his life had an interest in trousers. It's from politeness. It was because he didn't want to offend Isaac, whom he is avoiding, and he feels bad about it, but whom he'll avoid anyway. But now he has to get rid of these duds. He calls left and right, comes across a few of the intermediaries who have already participated in the deal that morning, and, because he doesn't have anywhere else to turn, calls an old acquaintance, Mr. Chéhonnay de Lopotte-Nadrague.*

This latter answers after only two rings; you'd think he was sitting by the phone waiting for Max's call.

"Hello, dear Monsieur, how are you? We don't see each other often enough. And how is Madame, your spouse? Her health? etc, etc., of course, etc., etc., and so forth, if I may. And how's business?"

"Well, on this matter, Monsieur Chéhonnay, I have an exceptional deal to offer you. This would also give us a good reason to get together again, to do lunch in that excellent restaurant in rue Bellechasse where we ate some time ago." And yadadi . . . without fail . . . and yadada . . . me too, and they finally, thank you and please, get to the gist of the matter.

"Only seventy francs apiece, though they're worth one hundred, on account of the material, the work, the style, the cut, the lining,

---

*The very French-sounding name is a pun on the Hungarian "pants thief." *Trans.*

the colors that are going to be fashionable this winter . . . They are O.Xi, a guarantee of quality in itself . . ."

Mr. Chéhonnay de Lopotte-Nadrague is convinced. He doesn't even argue for a second. We are among gentlemen, after all; a price is a price. They reach an agreement on the quantity, on the conditions of payment, on the delivery, on whether the truck should have a delivery ramp; they decide the date and place and the form of the contract that Max will have his secretary fax that very same day, and they agree to have lunch together the following week, in rue Bellechasse in the seventh arrondissement, the neighborhood of old wealth and old nobility, an arrondissement in which Max never sets foot and to which he doesn't remember how to go, and he wonders if he's going to need a visa, a passport, and a baptismal certificate to go for lunch . . .

The day after the delivery, Max gets a panicky phone call from Mr. Chéhonnay de Lopotte-Nadrague.

"Monsieur Max, the trousers were delivered as planned, the quantity was right, but there's a problem, a major one. Each trouser has only one leg! I checked the whole lot; the other leg is cut off at the knee! Monsieur Max, these trousers cannot be worn!"

Max observes a minute of pregnant silence, then answers his interlocutor, who is obviously and audibly in a state of shock.

"Monsieur Chéhonney, I think there's a deep misunderstanding here. I never told you these were pants to be worn. My dear Monsieur Chéhonnay, they're pants to be bought and sold."

THE RING

AT THE BAGHDAD MARKET, a long time ago, right after
the birth of duodecimal Shi'ism, in the time of the Abbassids, during the reign of Harun al-Rachid, before Saddam Hussein ("the
People's Benefactor"), before Hasan al Bakr ("the Good"), before
Marshall Aref ("the Gentle"), before General Kassem ("the Lover
of Peace"), before Abd Allah ("the Wise"), before Rashid'Ali ("the
Beloved"), before Faysal II ("the Friendly"), before Rhazi I ("the
Merciful"), before Ghazi ("the Friend of the Oppressed"), and before Faysal I ("the Shield of the Weak"), there were two shopkeepers at the great Baghdad bazaar. One was named Ahmed and was a
pious Muslim, while the other, Moshe, was a pious Jew. They were
friends; at this distant and improbable epoch of history, before Saddam Hussein the People's Benefactor, Hasan al Bakr the Good,
Aref the Gentle, Kassem the Lover of Peace, Abd Allah the Wise
and the other Beloved, Friendly, and Merciful had ruined, chased
away, massacred, exterminated the Jews. Before those times, these
latter, even though they were only second-class citizens, could live,
do business, and prosper in peace in the countries of sun, sand, and
algebra. Moshe's and Ahmed's respective stalls were at opposite
ends of the bazaar, a distance they doubly appreciated: on the one

hand, since they were both jewelers they could compete fairly without the animosity that too close proximity would have led to and, on the other, because the daily visit they paid each other gave them the excuse and opportunity to cross the whole bazaar from one end to the other, gleaning gossip, looking at the merchandise and prices, and getting an idea of the general ambiance.

In the course of one of his morning visits, Ahmed notices a silver ring on Moshe's stand, a superb ring with a sapphire. He is stunned by the ring, almost like love at first sight in front of two black eyes in a veiled face . . . This ring had a magical beauty.

"Oh, Moshe, this ring is magnificent. I just love it. I would like to buy it for myself. How much do you want for it?"

Moshe can't believe his ears. In the course of the many years they had known and appreciated each other they had never, but never, sold anything to each other. It didn't even cross their minds. But, why not after all?

"I would ask you ten dirhams," answers Moshe. "I am sure you would agree that it's worth a lot more, but since it is for you personally, and since you are like my brother, I am giving it to you for this ridiculous price."

Without saying another word, Ahmed pays the ten dirhams, puts the ring in his coin bag, bids Moshe good-bye, and quickly goes back to his shop and locks himself in to admire the wondrous ring in peace.

Moshe is astounded. Ahmed, a merchant and craftsman like him, had paid the asking price without negotiating, bargaining, quibbling, discussing, arguing, debating? This is unheard of in Baghdad's market.

"I must have just gotten myself shamefully robbed by Ahmed," thought Moshe. "This ring is worth one thousand times the price I asked him, and he is perfectly aware of it. That's not honest. And he calls himself my friend? Well, we shall see what we shall see!"

And without losing another minute, Moshe closes his shop and goes, or rather runs, to Ahmed's.

"Ahmed, the ring," he tells him out of breath, "the ring . . ."

"What about the ring?"

"I made a mistake; I forgot it was not for sale. My wife's father, you know him . . . I'll buy it back from you. How much do you want for it?"

Ahmed sees red, black. "Unbelievable!"

"Fifteen dirhams."

The Jew opens his coin bag in haste, quickly takes the ring, hides it, and goes away, running, like a thief.

Ahmed needs to sit down. The world must be coming to an end. A merchant, and what a merchant, Moshe himself! buys back at a loss merchandise he just sold! Without discussion, without bargaining.

"I was right. This ring is magical. It's priceless. Moshe sold it to me by mistake. And I, like an idiot, even though I had it in my possession, I resold it to him for a mere five dirhams in profit. Five dirhams! How could I have been such a donkey!"

Ahmed decided not to rush. The wait was horrible, unbearable. But he needed to be patient, to wait for the next day, and then drop by Moshe's stand casually while strolling, as if nothing was the matter.

This he does. After the customary greetings and inquiries, and while pretending not to care, Ahmed asks:

"Say Moshe, that ring, yesterday, you remember. [As if Moshe didn't remember. He too had not slept because of it the whole night.] I really did like it. Well, I liked it a bit . . . I have been thinking . . . I would like very much to have it. I am ready to buy it back from you, just like that, on a whim. You know whims can come over you from time to time . . . How much do you want for it?"

Moshe answers without wasting a second. He is ready, he has planned the whole thing. He's going to ask for a very large sum. Then he'll see if Ahmed wants to pay it—that would mean . . .

"One hundred dirhams."

"Here they are," says the Muslim.

And he goes away.

The two kept this up for weeks, then months. Taking turns, one after the other . . . The prices they paid reached incredible amounts. The whole bazaar knew about it. That ring had magical power.

One morning, it's Ahmed's turn to inquire about the ring.

"Good morning, Moshe . . ."

They go through the usual greetings . . . And then the matter at hand . . .

"The ring . . ."

"Well, Ahmed, I don't have it anymore. I sold it."

Ahmed feels faint. He leans on the wall of the shop. There's a silence that lasts an eternity, two eternities.

"You sold it? But Moshe, are you completely nuts? Have you lost your mind? You sold a ring our two families have been living off for the last six months?"

GOLF

R O B E R T   C O H E N , a liberal Belgian rabbi, loves to play golf. He's a "new style" rabbi, a modern one. He drives a car, owns a computer—and plays golf. How is it that he picked this sport for the gentry, for wealthy snobs? How did this son of poor and pious Moroccan Jews become first Reformed, then wealthy, then a golfer, and finally a Belgian? Only a psychoanalyst (and certainly not his parents) could explain it. But the fact remains, he loves this sport so much (and, I have to concede, he is a pretty good player) that he neglects many of his social and religious obligations to his synagogue and to the members of the community he is supposed to take care of.

For instance, this Saturday morning, a magnificent, sunny June morning with a light breeze tempering the heat of the sun . . . one of those mornings when one admires Creation, with a heart overflowing with joy—a joy that is a bit sensual, not quite appropriate for a rabbi, even a Reformed one—a morning in which thus, precisely, you feel the urge to thank the Creator for all things, and in particular for this world, so beautiful, so human.

But Cohen had no desire to thank the Creator in the place designated for this purpose, that is, the synagogue. He felt like enjoying this radiant morning in a different way and expressing his thanks to the Eternal God by taking advantage of the world He had put at his disposal.

He thus decides, in spite of the holy Sabbath, to go play a round on his favorite golf course. You're going to tell me: "It's not conceivable, it's completely impossible." I hear you. A rabbi . . . but this is a tale, no? In a tale, everything is allowed, everything is possible. So listen without interrupting me. Rabbi Cohen thus throws his *clubs,* his golfing shoes, and his other golfing attire in an elegant Lancel bag, gets in his car, and happily sets off for a distant rural suburb of Brussels at the very hour when the faithful are beginning to assemble for prayer. He knows it, but the pleasure he's seeking is more powerful than the attraction of serving God and his fellows. And, at any rate, he has made sure that no one in his neighborhood saw him leave, and that his Sabbath game would remain a secret to all his neighbors and acquaintances.

As he's thus driving, his hair and beard flowing in the wind (because, even though he is Reformed, he had let his beard grow, this more from male vanity than from conviction or contradiction), Satan, Lucifer, Mephisto, Mephistopheles, Beelzebub, the Devil, the Evil One, the Prince of Darkness, call him whatever you will, he's always the same, our familiar contradictor, our obscure self, sees him in his little red convertible and goes to tell the Lord.

"Look, look," says the delighted Evil One, "at what your favorite rabbi, your modern rabbi who understands everything, is doing on the day of the Sabbath, while the faithful are gathered in your house! Not only is he failing his duties, but moreover he is driving a car—and you know where? to play golf, can you imagine. And now, what are you going to do to him? What punishment will you inflict on this uncommon sinner who is breaking all of your rules, who's behaving no more as a rabbi than as a Jew?

But the Eternal God has no desire to make Satan happy—which shouldn't surprise you. He does nothing to the unaware Cohen. This latter, ignorant of the celestial dialogue, parks his little Spitfire in his reserved parking spot, hurriedly changes his clothes, and

runs to the course, whistling happily. There is no one to play with
him, but Cohen, usually so sociable, for once is happy to be alone.
He isn't particularly keen to be seen playing golf on the day of the
Sabbath . . .

Satan couldn't figure it out. He wouldn't have minded . . . but
the Lord? Satan was in a rage.

Cohen takes his *club* number (if you know how to play golf, you
must know with which club to begin the game—and if you are as ignorant as I am on these matters, you won't care anyway), and he
shoots the first ball straight into the hole. He'd made a hole in one.
He's a bit surprised. Even though he is a good player, he has only
very rarely hit the ball right away into the hole. Excellent beginning,
he thinks, and he starts on the second green: instant success; the
third, the same thing! The fourth green is a very difficult one, but
here again, he makes a hole in one. Cohen is getting dizzy. What's
going on? He never had such a score. He's beginning to be sorry
he's playing alone: no one can admire his incredible game, his superb strokes; no one can witness his victories. For a moment he
closes his eyes: he sees the small group of the faithful, most of them
his friends, in the house of the Lord where the priest is missing; he
sees, hears, Mr. Lebinski become agitated, yelling very loudly in
the ear of his deaf wife, but where is the rabbi? He imagines everyone, one by one in their usual seats . . . and he doesn't care. This vision that is so clear, almost photographic, gives him no remorse, no
sadness. Too bad. They'll all come back next week. In the mean-
while they're praying alone. Anyway, the *minyen,* the minimum re-
quirement of the presence of ten men, has surely been met as it is
every Saturday, so they can do the service without a leader—where
is it said that a leader must always be present? It's time to change
things. The sermon they needed, the word, he had already given to
them on Friday evening. Now let them open up a bit, let them be
free, let them express themselves by praying alone—hell, this is the
end of the twentieth century after all!

The denizen of the above-mentioned place is at that very moment looking down flabbergasted at all of Cohen's holes in one,

from the easiest green to the most tortuous one, and understands less and less the Lord, his inevitable boss-enemy-*alter ego.*

And Cohen, just as amazed, continues his triumphal march. He gets to a green that has always given him trouble in the past because of a clump of trees and the extra-long distance between the starting point and the hole, a hole so difficult that it is extremely rare for even the greatest champions to get it in four shots. He takes his special *club* in his hands, steadies his left foot, puts his weight on his right leg, lifts his *club,* twists his torso, and gives the ball the first of what he expects to be many strokes. The ball goes up high in the sky, whistles as it turns, flies off—much farther than could be possibly expected from Cohen's drive. This latter looks at it, stunned, as if he were looking at his red car and a comet waltzing together in the sky. His mouth hangs open; he drops his *club.* Then he starts to run as fast as he can, leaving his cart and his *clubs,* and sees the ball turn and pirouette in the sky. He sees it suddenly change direction, and fall straight into the ill-reputed hole. Cohen did it in a single, unique stroke! Never had anyone in the world since the time golf had been invented, no champion had ever ever succeeded in doing such a stunt! I'm the greatest golfer of all time! yells out Cohen. He exults, he overflows, he explodes.

Lucifer too explodes.

"How is it, cousin, that you allowed this miserable worm to have such a triumph? He just betrayed his studies, his profession, his faith (yours, between you and me), his friends, his flock (yours again), his community, and what have you, and you reward him by making him do the best hole in one of all time, a score you haven't given to the greatest champions who pray to you for hours on end in their churches before each meet? Can you explain this to me? Not only there's no punishment, but an extraordinary reward?"

The Lord looks at His old accomplice and tells him in a sweet and lively tone:

"No punishment? To whom do you suppose he'll be able to tell his story?"